麦格希 **中英双语阅读文库**

世界上最伟大的声音

第 **1** 辑

【美】 弗里德 (Freed, K.) ● 主编

刘慧 ● 译

麦格希中英双语阅读文库编委会 ● 编

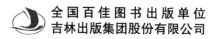

全国百佳图书出版单位
吉林出版集团股份有限公司

图书在版编目（CIP）数据

世界上最伟大的声音. 第1辑 / (美) 弗里德
(Freed,K.) 主编 ; 刘慧译 ; 麦格希中英双语阅读文库
编委会编. —— 2版. —— 长春 : 吉林出版集团股份有
限公司, 2018.3（2022.1重印）
（麦格希中英双语阅读文库）
ISBN 978-7-5581-4787-6

Ⅰ. ①世… Ⅱ. ①弗… ②刘… ③麦… Ⅲ. ①英语—
汉语—对照读物②演讲—世界—选集 Ⅳ. ①H319.4：I

中国版本图书馆CIP数据核字(2018)第046397号

世界上最伟大的声音　　第1辑

编：麦格希中英双语阅读文库编委会
插　　画：齐　航　李延霞
责任编辑：王芳芳
封面设计：冯冯翼
开　　本：660mm × 960mm　　1/16
字　　数：180千字
印　　张：9
版　　次：2018年3月第2版
印　　次：2022年1月第2次印刷

出　　版：吉林出版集团股份有限公司
发　　行：吉林出版集团外语教育有限公司
地　　址：长春市福祉大路5788号龙腾国际大厦B座7层
　　　　　邮编：130011
电　　话：总编办：0431-81629929
　　　　　发行部：0431-81629927　0431-81629921(Fax)
印　　刷：北京一鑫印务有限责任公司

ISBN 978-7-5581-4787-6　　定价：35.00元

前言 *PREFACE*

英国思想家培根说过：阅读使人深刻。阅读的真正目的是获取信息，开拓视野和陶冶情操。从语言学习的角度来说，学习语言若没有大量阅读就如隔靴搔痒，因为阅读中的语言是最丰富、最灵活、最具表现力、最符合生活情景的，同时读物中的情节、故事引人入胜，进而能充分调动读者的阅读兴趣，培养读者的文学修养，至此，语言的学习水到渠成。

"麦格希中英双语阅读文库"在世界范围内选材，涉及科普、社会文化、文学名著、传奇故事、成长励志等多个系列，充分满足英语学习者课外阅读之所需，在阅读中学习英语、提高能力。

◎难度适中

本套图书充分照顾读者的英语学习阶段和水平，从读者的阅读兴趣出发，以难易适中的英语语言为立足点，选材精心、编排合理。

◎精品荟萃

本套图书注重经典阅读与实用阅读并举。既包含国内外脍炙人口、耳熟能详的美文，又包含科普、人文、故事、励志类等多学科的精彩文章。

◎功能实用

本套图书充分体现了双语阅读的功能和优势，充分考虑到读者课外阅读的方便，超出核心词表的词汇均出现在使其意义明显的语境之中，并标注释义。

鉴于编者水平有限，凡不周之处，谬误之处，皆欢迎批评教正。

我们真心地希望本套图书承载的文化知识和英语阅读的策略对提高读者的英语著作欣赏水平和英语运用能力有所裨益。

丛书编委会

Contents

Love Your Life

—Henry David Thoreau

However mean your life is, meet it and live it; do not *shun* it and call it hard names. It is not so bad as you are. It looks poorest when you are richest. The *fault-finder* will find faults in *paradise*. Love your life, poor as it is. You may perhaps have some pleasant, thrilling, glorious hours, even in a poor-house.

热爱生活
——亨利·大卫·梭罗

不论你的生活如何卑贱，直面它，走下去，不要躲闪，更不要怨天尤人。生活远非你想的那么糟糕。富甲一方的生活也会看似贫瘠乏味。吹毛求疵的人就是给他天堂，他也会指指点点。因此即使你生活贫穷，也要热爱生活。即使生活在贫民收容所里，你也可能拥有舒服异常、欢呼雀跃和星光闪耀的时刻。

---

shun *v.* 避开；回避；避免

paradise *n.* 天堂

fault-finder *n.* 吹毛求疵的人

The setting sun is reflected from the windows of the alms-house as brightly as from the rich man's *abode*; the snow melts before its door as early in the spring. I do not see but a quiet mind may live as contentedly there, and have as cheering thoughts, as in a palace. The town's poor seem to me often to live the most independent lives of any. Maybe they are simply great enough to receive without *misgiving*. Most think that they are above being supported by the town; but it often happens that they are not above supporting themselves by dishonest means, which should be more *disreputable*. Cultivate poverty like a garden herb, like sage. Do not trouble yourself much to get new things, whether clothes or friends. Turn the old, return to them. Things do not change; we change. Sell your clothes and keep your thoughts.

　　无论是穷家陋室所，还是豪华别墅，窗上所反射的夕阳余晖都一样灿烂夺目；其门前的积雪也同样在早春时节融化。正所谓：知足者常乐，一个心绪宁静的人，无论身处何地都像生活在皇宫中一样快乐。城里的穷人看起来生活得最为潇洒自在，也许只是因为他们选择了接纳生活，而非殚精竭虑，怨天尤人。很多人都认为自己精明能干，从而拒绝城镇援助，然而事实则往往是他们常常眼高手低，不得不靠一些见不得光的手段谋生。因此，像圣人一般，视贫穷如园中之花而将之培育吧！不要刻意地追求新花样，衣服也好，朋友也罢。万物未变，唯有我们在变。衣服可以卖掉，但要保留你的思想。

---

abode *n.* 住所　　　　　　　　　　　　misgiving *n.* 担忧；疑虑
disreputable *adj.* 不光彩的

2

2

How to Be True to Yourself

—by Anonymous

When you know you're right, you can't back down. Always give others credit that is rightfully theirs. Don't be afraid of those who might have a better idea or who might even be smarter than you are.

Be honest and open about who you really are. People who lack genuine

如何对自己坦诚
——佚名

当你知道你做得对时，你就要勇往直前。

当别人值得赞扬，就赞扬他们！切莫害怕他人比你有更好想法或甚至比你更聪明。

真诚、坦率地展示真实的你。只有缺乏真正核心价值观的人才会为了自我感觉良好而依靠外在因素——相貌或社会地位。他们势必要竭尽所能

core values rely on external factors—their looks or status—in order to feel good about themselves. Inevitably they will do everything they can to preserve this facade, but they will do very little to develop their inner value and personal growth.

So be yourself. Don't engage in a personal *coverup* of areas that are unpleasing in your life. When it's tough, do it tough. In other words, face reality and be adult in your responses to life's challenges.

Self-respect and a clear conscience are powerful components of integrity and are the basis for enriching your relationships with others.

Integrity means you do what you do because it's right and not just fashionable or politically correct. A life of principle, of not *succumbing* to the *seductive sirens* of an easy morality, will always win the day.

来保全这种表面形象，但却很少去培养自己内在的价值和个人修为。

因此，要做自己，不要忙于掩盖生活中令人不快的方方面面。艰难的时刻更要顽强。换言之，要正视现实。面对生活的挑战，要老成持重、应对自如。

自尊和问心无愧是坦诚相待的有力组成部分，也是你拓展人脉的基石。

坦诚意味着你做某事是因为它是正确的，而不仅仅是为了赶时髦或在政治上无过失。坚持做事有原则，不屈于享乐的诱惑，这样的人生将会战无不胜。

---

coverup *n.* 掩盖

seductive *adj.* 有魅力的

succumb *v.* 屈从

siren *n.* 迷人的女人；妖妇

3

Adversity

—by Anonymous

There is no better school than adversity. Every defeat, every heartbreak, every loss, contains its own seed, its own lesson on how to improve my performance next time. Never again will I contribute to my downfall by refusing to face the truth and learn from my past mistakes. Because I know: gems cannot shine without polish, and I can not perfect myself without *hardship*.

逆境

——佚名

逆境是最好的一所学校。每一次失败、每一次打击，每一次失去都孕育着成功的萌芽，都教会我如何在下一次困境中表现得更出色。我不会逃避现实，也不会拒绝从往昔的错误中吸取教训，我更不会再因此而使自己一败涂地。因为我深知，玉不磨不成器，没有艰难险阻，就不会完善自我。

---

hardship *n.* 艰难；困苦

Now I know that there are no times in life when opportunity, the chance to be and do gathers so richly about my soul when it has to suffer cruel adversity. Then everything depends on whether I raise my head or lower it in seeking help. Whenever I am struck down, in the future, by any terrible defeat, I will inquire of myself, after the first pain has passed, how I can turn that adversity into good. What a great opportunity that moment may present... to take the bitter root I am holding and transform it into *fragrant* garden of flowers.

Always will I seek the seed of *triumph* in every adversity.

现在我知道，灵魂备受煎熬的时刻正是生命中选择与机会最富足的时刻。成功与否取决于我在寻求帮助时是昂首挺胸还是垂头丧气。将来无论何时，即使我被可怕的困难击倒，历经最初的苦痛之后，我也会想方设法将逆境变成转机。伟大的机遇就在此刻闪现……这苦涩的根必将换来满园芬芳！

我将在未来的每一次逆境中都探寻成功的萌芽。

---

fragrant *adj.* 芳香的　　　　　　　　　　　triumph *n.* 胜利；成功

4

I Am Powerful!

— by Anonymous

I am very powerful!

Whatever I set my mind on having, I will have.

Whatever I decide to be, I will be.

The evidence is all around me.

The power of my will has brought me *precisely* to where I am right now.

I have made the choices. I have held the thoughts.

我很强大！
——佚名

我很强大！

无论我的脑海里想拥有什么，我都将会拥有。

无论我决定将来何去何从，我都将会实现。

在我周围充斥着各种"我很强大"的证据。

意志的力量将我精确地带到了我当前所处之境地。

我已经做出了选择，我已经坚持了自己的想法。

precisely *adv.* 精确地

I have taken the actions to create my current reality.

And I have the power to change it into whatever I want it to be.

With the choices I make, I am *constantly* fulfilling the vision I have for my life.

If that does not seem to be the case—then I am *deceiving* myself about what I really want.

Because what I really, truly want, I will get!

What I truly wanted in the past, I already have.

If I want to build a billion-dollar business, I will take the actions necessary to do it.

If I want to sit comfortably watching TV night after night—

I will take the actions necessary for that.

我已经采取了行动来创造现实。

而且我有能力实现愿望。

随着选择的不断做出，我人生的蓝图也逐渐地清晰。

但如果结果并非如此——那么说明我一直在蒙蔽自己，不知道自己真正想要什么。

因为我真正想要的、真心想要的，我终会得到！

曾经我真正想要的，现在我已经拥有了。

如果我想创立一项10亿美元的生意，我会采取必要的行动来实现它。

如果我想夜复一夜舒舒服服地坐着看电视——我就会那样做！

---

constantly *adv.* 不断地　　　　　　　　　　　deceive *v.* 欺骗

Don't be disappointed in my results—they are just the outward *manifestation* of my *priorities*.

I will be sure of what I truly want, because I am sure to get it!

不要对我的结果失望——这只是我处理事件优先次序的表象。

我确信，我真正想要的，一定势在必得！

---

manifestation *n.* 表现   priority *n.* 优先事项；最重要的事

5

It's Never Too Late for Success (Excerpt)

—Charles D Rice

Y ou and your parents can stop worrying—Edison, Darwin and lots of more were far from being geniuses in their teens.

History books seldom mention it, but the truth is that many of our greatest figures were practically "beatniks" when they were teenagers. They were given to daydreaming, indecision, *hebetude*(plain dullness), and

---

成功永远不会太迟（节选）
——查尔斯·D·赖斯

你和你的父母不必再担忧——爱迪生、达尔文等许多人在青少年时代都与天才相差甚远。

虽然史书上很少提及，但实际上，许多杰出人物在少年时代都是不折不扣的"垮掉的一代"。他们被认定是异想天开、优柔寡断、反应迟钝（纯粹的呆笨），并且丝毫显示不出他们具备成为医生、律师或印第安酋长的潜力。

---

hebetude *n.* 迟钝；愚钝

they showed no promise of being a doctor, lawyer or Indian chief.

So, young men and women, if you suffer from the same *symptoms*, don't despair. The world was built by men and women whose parents worried that they would "never amount to a hill of beans". You don't hear too much about their early failures because parents prefer to cite more *inspiring* examples.

Charles Darwin's early life was a mess. He hated school, and his father once shouted: "You care for nothing but shooting dogs and rat catching, and you will be a disgrace to yourself and all your family!" He was sent to Glasgow to study medicine, but he couldn't stand the sight of blood. He was sent to *divinity* school and barely managed to graduate. Whereupon he chucked the whole business and shipped out to the South Seas on the famous exploring ship Beagle. On that voyage, one of history's greatest scientists was born. It was here that he collected the material for the book that

---

所以，年轻人，如果你身上也存在同样的症状，不要太失望。世界最初就是由这些曾令父母发愁且貌似一事无成的男女们建造的。关于他们早期的失败经历，你听到的也许并不多，因为父母总喜欢以一些鼓舞人心的事为例。

查尔斯·达尔文早年生活得一团糟。他讨厌上学，父亲曾冲他大发脾气喊道："你就知道猎狗捕鼠，你不光让自己丢脸还让全家人丢脸！"他曾被送到格拉斯哥学医，可他见不得血淋淋的场面。之后他又被送往神学院，结果勉强毕业。因此，他改弦易辙，乘坐闻名于世的"贝格尔"号考察船去了南太平洋。在那次航海期间，历史上最伟大的一位科学家诞生

---

symptom *n.* 征候；征兆　　　　　inspiring *adj.* 激励的；鼓舞人心的
divinity *n.* 神学

would *revolutionize* biological science—*The Origin of the Species*.

And added to all the *aforementioned* paradoxes you have a small army of child *prodigies* who graduated from college when they were 15, and are now obscure clerks in accounting departments. And you have a small army of men who were too stupid or indolent to get into or finish college and who are today presidents of the firms that hire the prodigies.

So who's to say what about youth? Any young boy or girl who knows what he/ she wants to do in life is probably better off for it. But no teenager needs despair of the future. He has that one special advantage over the greatest man alive—time.

了。正是在这里，他为将对生物科学进行变革的《物种起源》一书搜集了素材。

除了前面提到的怪才外，也许你还知道不少神童，他们15岁大学毕业，如今却是财务处的无名小卒；而当年过于愚钝或由于懒惰上不了大学或没能大学毕业的人现在竟成为雇佣这些神童的公司总裁。

因此，谁敢对年轻后生的前程妄下定论呢？任何一个确立人生目标的花季少年都很有希望功成名就，无论哪个花季少年都不要对未来失去信心。与健在人世的伟人相比，他们具备一个独特的优势——时间！

---

revolutionize *v.* 彻底改革   aforementioned *adj.* 前面提到的

prodigy *n.* 奇才；神通

6

Dance like No One Is Watching

—Tania Tyler

What a great philosophy to travel through life's journey with! It was interesting to receive this quote in an email this week as I have told many people "you just need to dance as though no one is watching." This statement can be taken *literally*—go out dancing and just let your spirit *soar*, enjoy yourself, have fun... Does it really matter what other's

跳舞吧，如同无人注视一样
——塔尼娅·泰勒

这是人生旅途中多么精辟的一条哲理啊！这句话是我这周在一封电子邮件中看到的，有意思的是，我也曾跟许多人说过："你们尽情去跳舞吧，如同无人观望一样。"这句话的字面意思是：去跳舞吧，让你的神采飞扬，尽情舞动，享受乐趣，享受生活……别人的想法真的很重要吗？我并不是说要推卸所有责任（毕竟我们生活在现实世界中），而是说要花一定的时间去探究真实的自我。我们要致力于寻求一

literally *adv.* 照字面地　　　　　　　　　　soar *v.* 高飞；翱翔

think? I'm not talking about throwing away all responsibilities (we do live in a real world), but rather about taking time to be or explore who we are. Work on finding a balance. Be true to yourself, and don't live your life to please others. Live to please yourself and others will be pleased. Emotions are *infectious*; why not spread happiness, joy and love?

Take the time to watch a *seagull* in flight. Some days, depending on the weather, they appear to just *float*, soar and really enjoy themselves. Watch again on a windy day, they have to work a little harder to get where they're going. Notice how when the weather gets stormy, they land and just hang out for a while. Here's a quote from "Jonathan Livingston Seagull" by Richard Bach: "Seagulls, as you know, never *falter*, never stall. To stall in the air is for them disgrace and it is dishonor. But Jonathan Livingston Seagull, unashamed,

---

种平衡：既要做真实的自己，又不必为取悦他人而活；为快乐而活，这样他人也会感到快乐。情绪是有感染力的，为何不将幸福、快乐、友爱传递给他人呢？

花些时间去观察一下飞翔的海鸥吧。它们的飞翔随天气而变，或者在海面上轻轻掠过，或者呼啸着飞向天际，无论如何，它们都很享受。在刮风时，它们必须更加用力地拍动翅膀才能飞到目的地。当狂风暴雨来临时，它们着陆后只逗留片刻。理查德·巴赫的《海鸥乔纳森·利文斯顿》中有这样一句话："如你所知，海鸥从不迟疑，从不停滞。在空中停滞对它们来说是耻辱，是件不光彩的事情。狂风暴雨中，海鸥乔纳森·利文斯

---

infectious *adj.* 有感染力的
float *v.* （使）漂浮

seagull *n.* 海鸥
falter *v.* 犹豫；畏缩

stretching his wings again in the trembling hard curve—slowing, slowing, and stalling once more—was no ordinary bird." Next time you get to a stormy day, read this book again as an adult. Everyday brings something new; learn to notice something new each day. Life will always be filled with challenges. Make the best of them. Enjoy life, and be happy. Go with the flow.

As we learn to "work like you don't need money", our jobs become less of a *burden* or struggle. Isn't life more pleasurable when you are doing something you enjoy rather than something you "have to"? Look upon work as something rewarding. Money isn't everything. Take pride in your tasks, be the best you can at what you do. Smile more. Try this for a couple of days; watch your

---

顿再一次坦然地张开翅膀——慢慢地，慢慢地，再一次停了下来——它是一只非同寻常的鸟。"在下一次狂风暴雨来临之际，作为一个成年人你需要再次阅读这本书。每一天都会有新的变化，因此每一天都要学习观察新的东西。生活永远充满着挑战，要学会充分把握。享受生活，开心快乐，随遇而安。

当我们学会"不为钱而工作"时，我们的工作就不会成为一种负担或挣扎。当你做自己喜欢的事而不是你"不得不"做的事情时，生活是不是更愉悦呢？视工作为回报。钱不是万能的。要为自己的工作感到骄傲，尽可能做到最好，多一点微笑。试着这样做几天，你会发现工作也是一

---

burden *n.* 负担

job transform into something more enjoyable. Chances are, more money will also come your way. Just imagine the difference in tips for a waiter/waitress who smiles and makes their job more enjoyable compared to the person that really doesn't want to be there. Or the possible job *promotions* when you put your best foot forward.

Take the time to enjoy life.

Time waits for no one...

件乐事。这样你将有机会获得更多的财富。试想面带微笑并以工作为乐趣的服务员，与着实不想留在那里的服务员相比，得到的小费肯定有所差别。全力以赴，尽心尽力，你或许会得到更多升职的机会。

抓紧时间享受生活吧。

时不待人……

---

promotion *n.* 晋升

7

Just for Today

—by Anonymous

Just for today I will try to live through this day only and not *tackle* my whole life problem at once. I can do something for twelve hours that would *appal* me if I had to keep it up for a lifetime.

Just for today I will be happy. This assumes to be true what Abraham Lincoln said, that "Most folks are as happy as they make up their minds to be."

只争朝夕
——佚名

只争朝夕，我将竭力活在当下而不是立刻着手解决终生的问题。即使这问题终生挥之不去，足以让我惊骇，我也只能坚持12个小时。

只争朝夕，我将很快乐。亚伯拉罕·林肯曾说过"大多数人都是想怎么高兴就怎么高兴。"此言不假。

---

tackle *v.* 解决

appal *v.* 使惊骇

Just for today I will *adjust myself to* what is, and not try to adjust everything to my own desires. I will take my "luck" as it comes.

Just for today I will try to strengthen my mind. I will study. I will learn something useful. I will not be a mental *loafer*. I will read something that requires effort, thought and *concentration*.

Just for today I will exercise my soul in three ways. I will do somebody a good turn and not get found out: If anybody knows of it, it will not count. I will do at least two things I don't want to do—just for exercise. I will not show anyone that my feelings are hurt: they may be hurt, but today I will not show it.

Just for today I will be agreeable. I will look as well as I can, dress becomingly, talk low, act *courteously*, criticize not one bit and try not to improve or regulate anybody but myself.

只争朝夕，我会调整自我适应现实，而不会强求万物以遂我心。既来之则安之，"听天由命"。

只争朝夕，我会充实自己。我会学习一些有用的东西，不做精神上的流浪汉。我会努力研读一些需要全神贯注、认真思索的书籍。

只争朝夕，我将采用以下三种方式来磨炼我的灵魂。一是助人而不为人知；二是至少要做两件自己不愿做但有用的事——哪怕只是为了磨炼自己；三是情感受伤不行于色，伤则伤矣，绝不表露。

只争朝夕，我将让自己看起来令人赏心悦目：容光焕发、穿着得体、谈吐斯文、举止优雅、决不吹毛求疵，尽量改进和调整自己，而不是别人。

---

adjust sb. to *使某人适应*   loafer *n. 游手好闲的人*
concentration *n. 专注；集中*   courteously *adv. 有礼貌地*

Just for today I will have a program, I may not follow it exactly, but I will have it. I will save myself from two *pests*: hurry and *indecision*.

Just for today I will have a quiet half hour all by myself and relax. During this half hour, sometime, I will try to get a better perspective of my life.

Just for today I will be unafraid. Especially I will not be afraid to enjoy what is beautiful, and to believe that as I give to the world, so the world will give to me.

只争朝夕，我会拟定计划。也许我不会严格照办，但不能没有。这将使我免于两大祸害：仓促行事和优柔寡断。

只争朝夕，我会抽出半小时独自静坐，彻底放松。此中某个时刻，我会找到更好的角度来审视我的生活。

只争朝夕，我将无所畏惧。尤其不再畏惧去享受美好的事物，并且坚信只要我对这世界有所付出，世界也一定会对我有所回报。

---

pest *n.* 讨厌的人（或物）　　　　　　　　indecision *n.* 优柔寡断

8

We Are Just Beginning

—by Anonymous

"We are reading the first *verse* of the first chapter of a book whose pages are *infinite*..."

I do not know who wrote those words, but I have always liked them as a reminder that the future can be anything we want to make it. We can take the mysterious, *hazy* future and carve out of it anything that we can imagine, just as a *sculptor* carves a

---

我们才刚刚开始
——佚名

"我们正在读一本书的第一章第一行，这本书很厚很厚……"

我不知道此言出于何处，可我很喜欢，它警示我们：未来由我们自己打造。未来神秘莫测，我们可以发挥想象，塑造自己的将来，犹如雕刻家运用他的想象力将未成形的石头雕刻成像。

---

verse *n.* 诗节
hazy *adj.* 模糊的

infinite *adj.* 无限的；无穷的
sculptor *n.* 雕刻家

statue from a shapeless stone.

We are all in the position of the farmer. If we plant a good seed, we reap a good harvest. If our seed is poor and full of *weeds*, we reap a useless crop. If we plant nothing at all, we harvest nothing at all.

I want the future to be better than the past. I don't want it *contaminated* by the mistakes and errors with which history is filled. We should all be concerned about the future because that is where we will spend the remainder of our lives.

The past is gone and static. Nothing we can do will change it. The future is before us and *dynamic*. Everything we do will affect it. Each day brings with it new *frontiers*, in our homes and in our business, if we only recognize them. We are just at the beginning of the progress in every field of human endeavor.

我们就像是农夫，撒下良种就会丰收，播下劣种或让农田杂草丛生便会徒劳无获。没有耕耘就没有收获。

我希望未来比过去更精彩，希望未来不要沾染历史的错误与过失。我们都应举目向前，因为我们要用余生书写未来。

往昔已逝，静如止水，我们无法去改变；而前方的未来正生机勃勃，我们所做的每一件事都将会影响着它。只要我们认识到这些，无论是在家中还是在工作上，每天我们的面前都会有新天地。在人类致力开拓的每一片领域上，一切才刚刚开始。

---

weed *n.* 野草　　　　　　　contaminate *v.* 玷污；污染
dynamic *adj.* 充满活力的　　frontier *n.* 新领域

Facing the Enemies Within

—— Jim Rohn

We are not born with courage, but neither are we born with fear. Maybe some of our fears are brought on by your own experiences, by what someone has told you, by what you've read in the papers. Some fears are *valid*, like walking alone in a bad part of town at two o'clock in the morning. But once you learn to avoid that situation, you won't need to live in fear of it.

直面内心的敌人
——吉姆·罗恩

勇气并不是与生俱来的，恐惧也不是。也许有些恐惧你曾亲身经历，也许有些是别人告诉你的，或者是你在报纸上读到的新闻。有些恐惧合情合理，譬如在凌晨两点独自走在城里不安全的地段。但是一旦你学会避免那种情况，你就不必生活在恐惧之中。

valid *adj.* 有效的

Fears, even the most basic ones, can totally destroy our ambitions. Fear can destroy fortunes. Fear can destroy relationships. Fear, if left unchecked, can destroy our lives. Fear is one of the many enemies lurking inside us.

Let me tell you about five of the other enemies we face from within. The first enemy that you've got to destroy before it destroys you is indifference. What a tragic disease this is! "Ho-hum, let it *slide*. I'll just drift along." Here's one problem with drifting: you can't drift your way to the mountain.

The second enemy we face is indecision. Indecision is the thief of opportunity and *enterprise*. It will steal your chances for a better future. Take a sword to this enemy.

The third enemy inside is doubt. Sure, there's room for healthy *skepticism*. You can't believe everything. But you also can't let doubt

---

恐惧，哪怕是最基本的恐惧，也可能彻底粉碎我们的雄心壮志。恐惧可能摧毁财富，也可能恶化感情。如果不加以遏制，恐惧还可能误人一生。恐惧是潜伏于我们内心的众多敌人之一。

让我来告诉你我们所面临的其他五个内在敌人。第一个是你要在它袭击你之前就将其击败的敌人——冷漠。譬如你打着哈欠说："随它去吧，让我随波逐流吧。"这是多么可悲的疾病啊！随波逐流的问题是：你不可能漂到山顶去。

我们面临的第二个敌人是优柔寡断。它是窃取机会和事业的小偷，它还会偷去你拥有美好未来的机会。向这个敌人亮剑吧！

第三个内在的敌人是怀疑。当然，正常的怀疑应该占据一席之地，

---

slide *v.* 滑动;滑行   enterprise *n.* 进取心
skepticism *n.* 怀疑态度

take over. Many people doubt the past, doubt the future, doubt each other, doubt the government, doubt the possibilities and doubt the opportunities. Worse of all, they doubt themselves. I'm telling you, doubt will destroy your life and your chances of success. It will empty both your bank account and your heart. Doubt is an enemy. Go after it. *Get rid of* it.

The fourth enemy within is worry. We've all got to worry some. Just don't let conquer you. Instead, let it alarm you. Worry can be useful. If you step off the curb in New York City and a taxi is coming, you've got to worry. But you can't let worry loose like a mad dog that drives you into a small corner. Here's what you've got to do with your worries: drive them into a small corner. Whatever is out to get you, you've got to get it. Whatever is pushing on you, you've got to

---

你不能相信一切，但是也不能让怀疑掌控一切。许多人怀疑过去，怀疑未来，怀疑彼此，怀疑政府，怀疑可能性，怀疑机会，最糟糕的是，他们还怀疑自己。我告诉你，怀疑会毁掉你的生活和你成功的机会；它会耗掉你的存款，留给你枯竭的心灵。怀疑是敌人，要驱赶它，消灭它。

第四个内在的敌人是忧虑。我们多多少少都会有些忧虑，不过千万不要让忧虑征服你。相反，要让它来警醒你。忧虑也许能派上用场。当你在纽约走上人行道时，一辆出租车向你驶来，你就会忧虑。但你决不能让忧虑像条疯狗一样失控而将你逼至死角。你应该把忧虑驱至死角。不管是什么来打击你，你都要击败它。不管是什么来攻击你，你都要反击回去。

---

get rid of 摆脱

push back.

The fifth interior enemy is overcaution. It is the timid *approach to* life. Timidity is not a virtue; it's an illness. If you let it go, it'll conquer you. Timid people don't get promoted. They don't advance and grow and become powerful in the market-place. You've got to avoid overcaution.

Do battle with the enemy. Do battle with your fears. Build your courage to fight what's holding you back, what's keeping you from your goals and dreams. Be courageous in your life and in your pursuit of the things you want and the person you want to become.

第五个内在的敌人是过分谨慎。那是怯懦的生活方式。怯懦不是美德，而是疾病。如果你放任它，它就会将你征服。怯懦的人不会主动提升，这样的人在市场中不会前进，不会成长，不会变得强大，因此你要避免过分谨慎。

一定要向敌人开战，一定要向恐惧开战。鼓起勇气向阻碍你进步的因素宣战，向阻止你实现目标和梦想的因素宣战。要勇敢地生活，勇敢地追求你想要的东西，勇敢地成为你想成为的人。

---

approach to　接近

10

Man's Guide

——Winston Leonard Spencer Churchill

Man in this moment of his history has emerged in greater *supremacy* over the forces of nature than has ever been dreamed of before. There lies before him, if he wishes, a golden age of peace and progress. He has only to conquer his last and worst enemy—himself.

The only guide to a man is his conscience; the only shield to his memory is the *rectitude*

人类的指导者

——温斯顿·伦纳德·斯宾塞·丘吉尔

如今，人类征服自然的力量空前强大，这是人类过去做梦都难以想到的。只要愿意，人类就可以创建一个和平与发展的黄金时代。然而他必须征服最后也是最险恶的一个敌人——自己。

唯一能指引一个人的是他的良知；追忆往事时唯一能保护他的盾牌是正直且真诚的行为。如果在人生的旅途中前行时不坚持此原则，实非明

supremacy　n.　至高无上　　　　　　　　　rectitude　n.　正直；公正

and *sincerity* of his actions. It is very *imprudent* to walk through life without this shield, because we are so often *mocked* by the failure of our hopes, but with this shield, however the fates may play, we march always in the ranks of honor.

We shall go forward together. The road upward is long. There are upon our journey dark and dangerous valleys, through which we have to make and fight our way. But it is sure and certain that if we persevere, and we shall persevere, we shall come through these dark and dangerous valleys into a sunlight broader and more genial and more lasting than mankind has ever known.

智之举，我们常常因为事与愿违而受到命运的嘲弄，但是借助于这样的为人之道，无论命运怎样跌宕起伏，至少在前行中总不会失去做人的尊严。

我们应该携手前进，前路漫漫。旅途中布满了幽暗危险的深谷，我们必须艰苦奋斗，自辟蹊径。但是可以肯定的是只要我们坚持不懈，也必须坚持到底，我们一定能够走出黑暗，穿越险境，到达一个前所未有、阳光普照、广阔无垠、生意盎然的光明世界。

---

sincerity *n.* 真诚   imprudent *adj.* 不明智的；不谨慎的
mock *v.* 嘲弄

11

If You Bring Love

— Joseph Campbell

At a certain moment in Nietzsche's life, the idea came to him of what he called "the love of your fate". Whatever your fate is, whatever the *heck* happens, you say, "This is what I need." It may look like a *wreck*, but *go at* it as though it were an opportunity, a challenge.

If you bring love to that moment—not discouragement—you will find the strength

如果爱下去
——约瑟夫·坎贝尔

尼采在他生命中的某一刻提出了"命运之爱"。无论你的命运如何，无论你的遭遇怎样，你都要说："这是命中注定。"这种观念也许看起来就像是将残骸视为机遇和挑战而竭力处之。

如果在那一刻选择爱下去——不气馁——你会找到激发你的力量。任何你能扛过的灾难，都可以将你的性格、身材和生活塑造得日臻完善。

---

heck *n.* <俚>（用以加强语气）到底；究竟　　　　wreck *n.* 残骸
go at 努力从事于

is there. Any disaster that you can survive is an improvement in your character, your *stature*, and your life. What a *privilege*! This is when the *spontaneity* of your own nature will have a chance to flow. Then, when looking back at your life, you will see that the moments which seemed to be great failures followed by wreckage were the incidents that shaped the life you have now. You will see that this is really true.

Nothing can happen to you that is not positive. Even though it looks and feels at the moment like a negative crisis, it is not.

这是何等的荣幸啊！这一刻正是你真情流露的机会呀。而后当你回首人生时，你会意识到正是那些曾经看似破烂不堪且极其失败的无数瞬间才造就了你现在的人生。你将领悟到这个事实千真万确。

　　凡事都有它积极向上的意义，即使这一刻看似糟糕透顶，而实则不然。

---

stature *n.* 身高；身材　　　　　　　　　privilege *n.* 荣幸；荣耀
spontaneity *n.* 自发行为

12

Positive Thought Positive Action

— Lana Keating

Positive thought is the action that needs to *take place* in order to have the law of attraction, which can produce positive results in your life. *Random* or negative thoughts result in negative or random unwanted results in your life.

Your thoughts, positive or negative, are your intention at the moment of that thought.

正面思考，积极行动
——拉纳·基廷

正面思考可以产生吸引力法则，从而对你的人生产生积极作用。任意妄为或消极的思想将让你的人生遭遇负面或不可预知的可怕后果。

无论你积极思索还是消极考虑，都是那一刻你的意向所在。

take place 发生

random adj. 随意的

The universe answers your intention and gives you what you think about the most. If your thoughts are negative you are going to receive negative results. Positive results are what we all want and positive or "good" thoughts produce a good result.

Is it really that simple on the face of it? However, the human being is the possessor of a only human *trait* called the ego. This trait is what produces the negative in us and the *ego* must be controlled or overcome every time a negative thought comes to the surface. And I am sure you know that this happens very often indeed.

Further, it seems that one positive thought is worth a great deal more than one negative thought otherwise we would have destroyed

天地万物会对你的意向给予应答并告诉你时刻萦绕于你心头的答案。如果你的想法消极，你将会承受负面影响。积极的成就是人所向往的，正面思考或"睿智哲思"总能善终。

难道这真的像表面上看起来的那么简单吗？然而，唯有人类才具备一种叫作自负的特质。这一特质使我们内心产生消极情绪，每一次当负面想法浮出水面时，我们必须控制或克服自负。而且我确信你知道这种情况的确会屡次出现。

再者，正面思考的价值似乎远超于消极想法，否则我们自开天辟地

trait n. 特征   ego n. 自我

each other or ourselves long ago. It seems to me that one positive thought can balance 100 negative thoughts. That makes our job easier by far.

Your positive thought *manifesting* as positive action can indeed change the world. You can save entire countries and entire populations with only one small act. You must stay alert to positive opportunities which may be as small as a smile or as large as *hauling* someone out of a car wreck.

The choice is yours as is every thought and action you perform. Make it a positive one, go ahead to save the world.

之日起就开始自相残杀或自我摧残了。依我之见，一次正面思考可以抵上一百种消极想法。显然这使我们的工作更轻而易举。

正面思考，积极行动，的确可以改变世界。仅通过一个小小的举动你就能够挽救整个国家和全体人民。对于积极行动的机会你必须保持警觉，即使这个机会小到一个微笑或大到把一个人拖离车祸现场。

每一个想法，每一次行动都取决于你自己。选择正面思考，积极行动，勇往直前地去拯救世界吧！

---

manifest *v.* 显露   haul *v.* 拖；拉

You Are So Powerful!

—Lana Keating

You have so much power in you... power to *accomplish* anything you want. Do you doubt that?

If you do, think about this. What type of body molecules do you suppose bicyclist Lance Armstrong has that you don't have? Your brain is made up of the same type of tissue Armstrong's brain has. Your heart has the same type of tissue. The same

---

你是如此强大！

——拉纳·基廷

你拥有如此强大的内在力量……足以实现你一心向往的愿望。难道你对此有疑问吗？

着手做某事时，不妨想想这句至理名言吧。自行车运动员兰斯·阿姆斯特朗的身体拥有什么异于常人的分子结构类型吗？你们的大脑都是由相同类型的组织组成，心脏也是如此。同理可证，生意如此成功的比尔·盖茨也和你拥有同样的身体构成。

---

accomplish *v.* 完成

would hold true for a business success like Bill Gates.

You have a completely different body than Armstrong or Gates. That has always been true, but today DNA would prove that. But your mind has the same ability these two people have displayed. They dreamed, followed through with that dream, and achieved great things. They knew what they wanted to do with their lives. They had a vision of what they wanted to accomplish. And they never let go of that dream.

It's never wise to compare yourself to someone you admire, saying they have something you don't have. *Comparison* is never good. If you haven't accomplished what you hoped you would, it's not because you are *inadequate* in any way. You have what it takes. You've always had it!

Use your power. Follow your dream, no matter how large. Go for it!

你拥有一个完全不同于阿姆斯特朗或盖茨的身躯，这千真万确，并且今天的DNA也会证实这一点。但是你们的脑海里却具备相同的才能。他们放飞梦想，努力追随，而后成就伟业。他们都知道生命的真谛，都拥有一个迫切实现的梦想，并且从来都没有放弃过这个梦想。

将你钦佩的人与自己形成对比，慨叹他们拥有而你却无法拥有的东西向来都不是明智之举。比较未必就是好事一桩。如果你没有实现你所希望的梦想，这并不表示你有任何不足之处。你具备实现梦想所需要的一切。你一直都拥有！

凭借你一己之力，无论梦想有多大，都要努力追随。加油前进吧！

---

comparison *n.* 比较；对照　　　　inadequate *adj.* 不充足的；不适当的

14

Religio Medici (Section II)

— Sir Thomas Browne

It is my *temper*, and I like it the better, to affect all *harmony*: and sure there is music even in the beauty, and the silent note which Cupid strikes, far sweeter than the sound of an instrument. For there is a music where ever there is a harmony, order, or proportion: and thus far we may maintain the music of the Sphears; for those well-ordered motions, and regular paces, though

虔诚的医生（第二章节）
——托马斯·布朗

我生性深爱一切之和谐，于此，我颇以自得；确实，甚至在丘比特所演奏的无声音籁与美感之中，音乐都无处不在，其吐音之妙凌驾于一般乐器之上。此亦因音乐处于和谐、秩序与比例匀称之中，而星际乐声一说至少可以因此而立足；其秩序井然之动作，节拍分明之步调，虽在常人耳中悄无声息，然而在颖慧者听来，此乃饱含和谐之妙乐。

temper n. 脾气   harmony n. 和谐

they give no sound unto the ear, yet to the understanding they strike a note most full of harmony. Whatsoever is harmonically composed delights in harmony; which makes me much distrust the *symmetry* of those heads which declaim against all Church-Musick. For myself, not only for my *obedience*, but my particular Genius, I do embrace it: for even that vulgar and Tavern-Musick, which makes one man merry, another mad, strikes in me a deep fit of devotion, and a profound *contemplation* of the First Composer. There is something in it of Divinity more than the ear discovers: it is an *hieroglyphical* and shadowed lesson of the whole World, and creatures of GOD; such a melody to the ear, as the whole World, well understood, would afford the understanding. In brief, it is a sensible fit of that harmony which intellectually sounds in the ears of GOD.

大凡构成和谐之物，必喜和谐，据此，则彼辈攻击一切教堂音乐者，其头脑之中是否尚有匀称二字，我深表疑虑。至于我自己，我对上述之音乐确实心悦诚服，固然与我虔诚之信仰息息相关，亦由我的特殊禀赋所致；甚至旅店的俚俗之乐，都饱含着欢乐狂热之情，都使我对最初的作曲家顿生仰慕之情与深刻冥想；其神圣之处非人耳所能察觉。它是茫茫世界和芸芸众生中一条朦胧难懂的经验教训，待众人大彻大悟而供知音聆听的悠扬妙乐。简而言之，它是响彻天际、玲珑曼妙的和谐之音。

---

symmetry *n.* 对称；匀称
contemplation *n.* 沉思

obedience *n.* 服从；顺从
hieroglyphical *n.* 象形文字

Afraid to Risk?

— Steve Goodier

An old poem by Richard Armour makes a good point:

The bride, white of hair, is *stooped* over her cane.

Her faltering footsteps need guiding.

While down the church *aisle*, with wan toothless smile,

The groom in a wheelchair comes riding.

And who is this elderly couple you ask?

害怕风险吗?

——史蒂夫·古德尔

首由理查德·爱默所作的古诗阐述了精辟独到的见解:

白发苍苍的新娘佝偻着身躯,倚着拐杖,

她步履蹒跚,还需要搀扶引路。

通道里,没有牙齿却洋溢着略显苍白微笑的新郎,

坐着轮椅自信前来。

你会问这对老夫妇是谁?

---

stoop *v.* 弯腰　　　　　　　　　　aisle *n.* 纵直通道;走道

You'll find, when you've closely explored it,

That here is that rare, most conservative pair,

Who waited until they could afford it.

Are you ever afraid to take a risk? Afraid to commit because of an uncertain future? Afraid of failing? Not that anyone would wait an entire life before taking a chance on marriage, but do you tend to wait until all possible risks are minimized before setting out in a new direction?

Though caution and common sense are certainly important, sometimes a risk is called for. As the late William Arthur Ward wisely said:

To laugh is to risk appearing a fool.

To weep is to risk appearing *sentimental*.

To reach out for another is to risk involvement.

当你仔细观察后，你就会发现，
他们就是这里极为罕见且最最保守的，
  一直等到能担负起婚姻的那一对夫妻。
  你曾经畏惧冒险吗？是否曾因为不可预测的未来而不敢去承诺？是否曾担心失败？不是每个人都在拥有婚姻的机会前而穷极一生去等待，但是难道你会倾向于等待，直到在开辟出新的方向之前将所有可能的风险减至最低？
  谨慎和常识固然重要，但是有时需要冒险。正如已故的威廉·阿瑟·沃德的睿智之语：
  想欢笑，就会冒险暴露你的无知。

---

sentimental *adj.* 多愁善感的

To expose feelings is to risk revealing your true self.

To place you ideas, your dreams, before a crowd is to risk rejection.

To love is to risk not being loved in return.

To live is to risk dying.

To hope is to risk disappointment.

To try is to risk failure.

But risks must be taken, because the greatest *hazard* in life is to risk nothing.

想哭泣，就会冒险暴露你的脆弱。

想与他人交往，就会冒险被牵连其中。

想吐露心声，就会冒险暴露真我。

想当众谈及你的见解，你的梦想，就会冒险遭到奚落。

想爱，就会冒险不会有同等的爱来回报。

想生存，就会冒险遭遇死亡的来临。

想希望，就会冒险领略失望。

想尝试，就会冒险遭遇失败。

但是，必须敢于冒险，因为生活中最大的危险是不敢冒险。

---

hazard *n.* 危险

Those who risk nothing, do nothing, have nothing, and become nothing.

They may avoid present suffering and sorrow, but they will not learn, feel, change, grow, love, or live.

Chained by their fear, they are slaves who have forfeited their freedom.

Only a person who risks is free.

The *pessimist* complains about the wind;

The *optimist* expects it to change;

And the realist adjusts the sails.

Is fear preventing you from taking a necessary risk today?

那些不勇于冒险的人，终将会无所事事，一无所有，仅成为一个无足轻重的人。

他们也许逃避了此刻的痛苦和悲伤，但是却不会从中学习、感受、改变、成长、关爱或生活。

被恐惧束缚着，他们俨然已经成为丧失自由的奴隶。

只有敢于冒险的人才能自由自在。

悲观主义者抱怨风向；

乐观主义者静观其变；

现实主义者调整风帆。

今天恐惧阻止你去冒险了吗？

---

pessimist *n.* 悲观主义者   optimist *n.* 乐观主义者

We Are the Decent People

—— Wilferd A. Peterson

We are the *decent* people of the world. We are in the majority, for men and women are essentially decent. We live in all nations, we live under all the flags that fly.

Decency is not determined by our economic status, our *religion*, the language we speak, the color of our skin, or the *ideology* under which we live. Human decency is a universal quality.

我们是正义之士
——威佛德·A·派特森

我们是世间的正义之士。我们是世上的主流，因为不论男女，就其本质而言都是正义之士。我们代表着各个民族，居住在各自国家飘扬的国旗下。

正义并不取决于我们的经济地位、宗教信仰、语种、肤色，或是意识形态，正义是人类共有的一种品质。

---

decent *adj.* 正派的   religion *n.* 宗教
ideology *n.* 意识形态；思想方式

We, the decent people of the world, often have our voices *drowned out* by the shouts of leaders who misrepresent the things for which we stand.

We, the decent people, carry enough weight to tip the scale for decency if we will make ourselves heard...

We believe that war is the great indecency, that it kills and destroys all the higher sensibilities of man and leaves only death, suffering, and destruction in its wake.

We believe that this is a beautiful universe and that it is made for love and not for hate; for peace and not war; for freedom and not slavery; for order and not *riot*; for *compassion* and not violence; for happiness and not misery.

We believe that there is only one war to be waged in the name of

---

作为世间正义之士，我们的呼声常常被那些歪曲我们立场的权势之人的大呼小叫声所淹没。

如果我们这些正义之士想让世人听到我们的呼声，我们就要有足够的力量去争取大规模的正义。

我们坚信，战争毫无正义可言，它会吞噬并泯灭人类所有的高尚情感，留下的只有死亡、灾难和毁灭。

我们坚信，这美丽世界的存在是为了爱，而非恨；是为了和平，而非战争；是为了自由，而非奴役；是为了秩序，而非暴乱；是为了仁慈，而非暴力；是为了幸福，而非痛苦。

我们坚信，只有一种战争的发起可以以人类正义之名，那就是为了消

---

drown out　（声音）淹没（另一声音）　　　　　　riot　n.　暴乱；骚乱
compassion　n.　同情；怜悯

human decency, and that is the war against all the common enemies of man... hunger, disease, poverty, ignorance, crime and failure.

We believe that every child should have the chance to grow up in an *atmosphere* of faith, not of fear.

We believe that the ultimate decency is to help men and never harm men, to lift men and not degrade men, and to respect the dignity of all men as individual human beings.

We, the decent people of the world stand, for the kind of life that will be good for all of the people, all of the time, everywhere.

灭人类共同的敌人而战……饥饿、疾病、贫穷、无知、犯罪和失败。

我们坚信，所有的孩子都应有机会成长在一个充满信任而非恐惧的氛围之中。

我们坚信，正义最终是为了帮助人类，而绝非伤害；为了提升人类，而非羞辱；为了像尊重个人一样尊重所有人的尊严。

作为世间的正义之士，我们无论何时，何地，都会倡导有益于人类的生活方式。

---

atmosphere *n.* 气氛；氛围

17

On Achieving Success

——Ernest Hemingway

We cannot travel every path. Success must be won along one line. We must make our business the one life purpose to which every other must be *subordinate*.

I hate a thing done by halves. If it be right, do it boldly. If it be wrong, leave it undone.

The men of history were not *perpetually*

关于获得成功

——欧内斯特·海明威

我们不可能走遍所有的路，只有执着于一条道路才能获得成功。因此，我们必须有一个终生追求的目标，其他的则从属于这个目标。

我痛恨做事半途而废。如果这件事是正确的，则勇往直前，大胆去做；如果这件事不对，就毅然放弃。

在历史长河中，伟人并不是靠终日观瞻镜中的自己来衡量自身形象，

---

subordinate *adj.* 从属的；次要的   perpetually *adv.* 持久地；永恒地

44

looking into the mirror to make sure of their own size. Absorbed in their work they did it. They did it so well that the wondering world sees them to be great, and *labeled* them accordingly.

To live with a high ideal is a successful life. It is not what one does, but what one tries to do, that makes a man strong. "Eternal *vigilance*," it has been said, "is the price of liberty". With equal truth it may be said, "Unceasing effort is the price of success". If we do not work with our might, others will; and they will *outstrip* us in the race, and pluck the prize from our grasp.

Success grows less and less dependent on luck and chance. Self-distrust is the cause of most of our failures.

The great and indispensable help to success is character. Character is a crystallized habit, the result of training and

---

而是来自于对事业的全心投入与不懈追求。因此，芸芸众生视他们卓越非凡，并称他们为伟人。

为崇高的理想而活就是一种成功，使人变强大的，不是这个人做了什么，而是他努力尝试去做什么。有人说过，"恒久的警惕是自由的代价"，那同样也可以说，"不懈的努力是成功的代价"。倘若我们不全力以赴地工作，别人会全力以赴，随后他们会在竞争中超越我们，从我们手中夺取胜利的果实。

成功越来越不依赖于运气和巧合，丧失自信是我们失败的主要原因。

性格是取得成功不可或缺的助力。性格是一种固化成形的习惯，是不

---

label *v.* 贴标签
outstrip *v.* 超过；胜过

vigilance *n.* 警戒；警觉

conviction. Every character is influenced by *heredity*, environment and education. But these apart, if every man were not to be a great extent the architect of his own character, he would be a *fatalist*, and irresponsible creature of circumstances.

Instead of saying that man is a creature of circumstance, it would be nearer the mark to say that man is the architect of circumstance. From the same materials one man builds palaces, another hovel. Bricks and *mortar* are mortar and bricks, until the architect can make them something else.

The true way to gain much is never to desire to gain too much. Wise men don't care for what they can't have.

断培养并坚信某事的结果。每个人的性格都会受到遗传因素、环境因素和教育因素的影响。但除此之外，如果人在很大程度上不能成为自己性格的构筑者，那么他就会沦为宿命论者，从而成为环境的失败产物。

与其说人是环境的产物，不如说人是环境的建筑师更贴切些。同样的材料，有人能用其建造出宫殿，而有人只能建成简陋的小屋。在建筑师将其变成建筑之前，砖泥依然是砖泥。

要想得到的多，就永远不要奢望太多。智者，不会在意他们得不到的东西。

heredity *n.* 遗传；遗传性　　　　　　　　　　fatalist *n.* 宿命论者
mortar *n.* 砂浆；灰浆；胶泥

18

Life Is Worthwhile

— Jim Rohn

Life Tip (1)

First, life is worthwhile if you LEARN. What you don't know will hurt you. You have to have learning to exist, let alone succeed. Life is worthwhile if you learn from your own experiences, *nega-tive* and positive. You learn to do it right by first sometimes doing it wrong.

让生活更有意义
——吉姆·罗恩

忠告 1

首先，如果你肯学，生活就有意义。无知害人不浅。别说是成功，就连生存你都需要去学。如果你肯从亲身经历中吸取经验教训，无论成功与否，你的生活都会别具一格。我们可从第一次做错事中学会如何正确处事，这就是所谓的好坏兼备。我们也应从别人的经历中吸

---

negative *adj.* 消极的

We call that a positive negative. We also learn from other people's experiences, both positive and negative. I've always said it is too bad that failures don't give *seminars*. We don't want to pay them so they don't tour around giving seminars. But the information would be very valuable—how someone who had it all, messed it up. Learning from other people's experiences and mistakes.

We learn by what we see—pay attention, by what we hear—be a good listener. Now I do suggest being a selective listener, don't just let anybody *dump* into your mental factory. We learn from what we read. Learn from every source. Learn from lectures, learn from songs, learn from sermons, learn from conversations with people who care. Keep learning.

取经验教训，不管成败与否。我总是说，失败者不举办研讨会真是太遗憾了。显然，我们不想花钱听人讲失败的经历，因此他们也就不会到处举办研讨会。然而那些信息却非常宝贵——我们可以从中得知某个曾经春风得意的人后来如何变得一团糟。我们可以从他人的经历或失误中开始学着变乖。

我们可通过眼见之事来学习——故要留心观察；可通过耳闻之事来学习——故要用心倾听。但在此我建议你一定要有选择地倾听，不要随便往你的"大脑工厂"里倾倒垃圾。从读书中学，从各种信息来源中学，从演讲中学，从歌曲中学，从训诫中学，从与别人的交谈中学。学无止境。

---

seminar *n.* 研讨会   dump *v.* 倾倒；倾斜

Life Tip (2)

Life is worthwhile if you TRY. You can't just learn; you now have to try something to see if you can do it. Try to make a difference, try to make some progress, try to learn a new skill, try to learn a new sport. Life is worthwhile if you try. It doesn't mean you can do everything but there are a lot of things you can do, if you just try. Try your best. Give it every effort. Why not go all out?

Life Tip (3)

Life is worthwhile if you STAY. You have to stay from spring until harvest. If you have signed up for the day or for the game or for the project—see it through. Sometimes *calamity* comes and then it is worth wrapping it up. And that's the end, but just don't end in the

---

忠告（2）

如果你尝试，生活就有意义。你不能光学不练，你还要去小试牛刀，看看你是否能做到。试着去改变，试着去进步，试着去学一门新技能，试着去学一项新运动。如果你尝试，生活就有意义。这并不意味着你可以做成任何事，但是只要你尝试，你就可以做成很多事。尽你所能，做到最好。为什么不全力以赴呢？

忠告（3）

如果你坚持，生活就有意义。你必须从春天坚持到秋收。如果你已经定好一天的日程，或定好参加某项赛事或某个项目——坚持下去。有时

---

calamity *n.* 灾难；极大的不幸

middle. Maybe on the next project you pass, but on this one. If you signed up, see it through.

Life Tip (4)

Life is worthwhile if you CARE. If you care at all you will get some results, if you care enough you can get incredible results. Care enough to make a difference. Care enough to turn somebody around. Care enough to start a new *enterprise*. Care enough to change it all. Care enough to be the highest producer. Care enough to set some records. Care enough to win.

灾难会降临，但是坚持下去绝对值得。坚持到底，不要半途而废。也许你会错失下一个项目，但是对于目前这个，如果你已做出承诺，就应坚持下去。

忠告 （4）

如果你在意，生活就有意义。如果你在意一切，你就会有所收获；如果你足够在意，你会收获意想不到的效果。足够在意会让人有所改变，足够在意也会让某人回心转意，足够在意创办的新企业，足够在意彻底的改变，足够在意成为最高级别的制造商，足够在意打破纪录，足够在意去赢。

---

enterprise *n.* 企业

What I Have Lived For

—— Bertrand Russell

Three passions, simple but *overwhelmingly* strong, have governed my life: the longing for love, the search for knowledge, and unbearable pity for the suffering of mankind. These passions, like great winds, have blown me hither and thither, in a wayward course, over a deep ocean of anguish, reaching to the very verge of despair.

I have sought love, first, because it brings

我为何而生

——白特兰·罗素

对爱情的无比渴望，对知识的孜孜追求，对人类苦难不可遏制的同情，这三种简单而又极其强烈的情感支配了我的一生。这些情感犹如劲风，将我尽情地吹向四方，掠过深沉苦痛的大海，直抵绝望的边缘。

我追寻爱，首先，因为爱情使我心为之着迷——这种美妙的沉醉竟使我愿意用余生去换取哪怕几个小时这样的喜悦。我追寻爱，其次，因为爱

---

overwhelmingly *adv.* 极强烈地；势不可挡地

ecstasy—ecstasy so great that I would often have sacrificed all the rest of my life for a few hours for this joy. I have sought it, next, because it relieves loneliness—that terrible loneliness in which one shivering consciousness looks over the rim of the world into the cold unfathomable lifeless abyss. I have sought it, finally, because in the union of love I have seen, in a *mystic miniature*, the *prefiguring* vision of the heaven that saints and poets have imagined.This is what I sought, and though it might seem too good for human life, this is what—at last—I have found.

With equal passion I have sought knowledge. I have wished to understand the hearts of men. I have wished to know why the stars shine... A little of this, but not much, I have achieved.

Love and knowledge, so far as they were possible, led upward toward the heavens. But always pity brought me back to earth.

情可以让我摆脱孤独——那种可怕的孤独，犹如一个颤抖的灵魂立于世界的边缘，而摆在面前的是冰冷、无底的死亡深渊。我追寻爱，最后，在爱的交融中，我仿佛看到了古今圣贤以及诗人们所向往的天堂之缩影，这正是我所追寻的人生境界，虽然对人的一生而言似乎有些遥不可及，但至少是我穷极一生所领悟到的真谛。

我曾以同样的激情探求知识，我渴望去了解人类的心灵，也渴望知道群星闪烁的缘由……我已经领略一二，尽管寥寥无几。

爱情与知识，总是凭借其能量将人类引向天堂。可对人类苦难的同情却总是把我拽到尘世之中。那些痛苦的哭喊经常在我内心深处回荡。忍饥

---

ecstasy *n.* 狂喜
miniature *n.* 微型复制品

mystic *adj.* 神秘的
prefigure *v.* 预示；预兆

Echoes of cries of pain *reverberated* in my heart. Children in famine, victims *tortured* by oppressors, helpless old people a hated burden to their sons, and the whole world of loneliness, poverty, and pain make a mockery of what human life should be. I long to alleviate the evil, but I cannot, and I too suffer.

This has been my life. I have found it worth living, and would gladly live it again if the chance were offered me.

挨饿的孩子，受压迫摧残的苦难者，被子女视为增加负担的无助老人，以及充满无尽孤独、贫穷和痛苦的整个世界，使人类所应有的生活成为笑柄。我常常希望能尽自己的绵薄之力去减少邪恶，但是我无能为力，因为我自己也难逃其折磨。

这就是我的一生，我已然发现人生的价值。如果再给我一次重生的机会，我将欣然接受这难得的赐予。

reverberate *v.* 回响　　　　　　　　　torture *v.* 使痛苦

20

Windows of Light

—Joseph H. Friend

Let there be many windows to brighten your soul.

Let the light shine through and touch your heart.

Bringing you hope, faith and love— the *purity* of grace within the *corridors* of yourself.

The *thorns* of life look for someone to soothe their cares and lift their thoughts.

光之窗

——约瑟夫·弗伦德

让更多窗来照亮你的灵魂。
让闪耀的光芒照射至你心灵深处，
带给你希望、信念和爱——纯洁优雅且由内而发的魅力。
在荆棘丛生的生活中寻觅那个能够减轻烦恼和消除顾虑的人。
繁星往往暗夜中才会闪烁，所有曾迷失的也将得以返还。

---

purity *n.* 纯洁   corridor *n.* 走廊；通道
thorn *n.* 荆棘；棘

Stars will blossom in the darkness, all losses are restored. Hope is the anchor of yourself, an incentive of achievement.

Every tomorrow has two faiths.

One is putting faith to work. The other is prayer.

Prayer frees us from the troubles we fear and gives us strength and courage to continue.

It becomes the guide book to happiness.

Faith gives one the courage to face the future with *expectancy*, assuring protection and enabling to *make peace with* our past.

The power of your mind has healing abilities and *self-esteem* in gaining control of your life.

So open the blinds in your thoughts, allow the sunshine to pour

希望是你自己抛出的锚，激励着你功成名就。

每一个明天都有两份信念。

一份用于执念工作。另一份用于虔诚祈祷。

祈祷帮助我们挣脱我们所恐惧的困境，赋予我们勇往直前的力量和勇气。

它成为快乐指南。

信念赋予我们面对未来的勇气，并保护我们，使未来与过去和睦相处。

意识的力量在掌控人生方面能够自我治愈及自我尊重。

因此打开思想之窗，让阳光倾注心中，与你所爱的人分享你的勇气。

expectancy *n.* 期待　　　　　　　make peace with 同……讲和
self-esteem *n.* 自尊

into your heart, and share your courage with your loved ones.

Regret taxes the soul. Today is all yours. Use it well.

Faith and hope are beautiful words.

When there is doubt, have faith. When there is despair, have hope.

When there is darkness, remember light follows night into joys of a new beginning.

Never let it be *separated.*

Have the courage to face the truth.

遗憾需要灵魂付出代价。今天你可以尽情欢畅。好好把握。

信念和希望是美丽的辞藻。

当存有疑虑时，请坚持信念。当绝望侵袭时，请充满希望。

当黑暗降临时，请牢记光芒会紧随夜幕之后，跨入到崭新开始的喜悦之中。

绝不让它离去。

勇敢面对现实。

---

separate *v.* 分开

It will strengthen your belief and make your life sweet, *serene* and most satisfying.

In sharing this essay with you, it is my hope that it will help people along their life's journeys.

To benefit not only themselves, but to comfort others along their way.

Bless you and be well.

坚定信念，生活将变得甜美、宁静和让人心满意足。

在分享这篇散文时，我希望在人生之旅中，此文能够有所裨益。

不仅为了有益于我们自己还可以在旅途中慰藉他人。

祝福你万事如意。

---

serene *adj.* 宁静的

21

Set Yourself Free

— Edmund O'Neill

Set yourself free from anything that might *hinder* you in becoming the person you want to be. Free yourself from the uncertainties about your abilities or the worth of your dreams, from the fears that you may not be able to achieve them or that they won't be what you wanted.

随心所欲

——埃德蒙·奥尼尔

随心所欲，挣脱任何可能妨碍自己实现理想的束缚。不要因为可能实现不了就怀疑自己的能力，也不要因为对自己的梦想毫无把握就否定了它的价值。

hinder *v.* 阻碍；妨碍

Set yourself free from the past. The good things from yesterday are still yours in memory; the things you want to forget you will, for tomorrow is only a sunrise away. Free yourself from regret or guilt, and promise to live this day as fully as you can.

Set yourself free from the *expectations* of others, and never feel guilty or embarrassed if you do not live up to their standards. You are most important to yourself; live by what you feel is best and right for you. Others will come to respect your integrity and honesty.

Set yourself free to simply be yourself, and you will soar higher than you've ever dreamed.

随心所欲，挣脱过去的束缚。昨天的美好事物仍然会驻足在你的记忆中；忘记想要忘记的，因为明天又是崭新的一天。不要遗憾，不要愧疚，只需竭尽所能地今朝有酒今朝醉，让生活更充实。

随心所欲，挣脱别人对自己的期望，即使达不到别人的标准，也不要因此而感到内疚或不安。于你而言，自己的感受才最重要；按照你的执念去生活才是适合你的最佳方式。别人随之也会钦佩你的正直和诚实。

随心所欲，简简单单做自己，你将超越梦想，飞得更高。

---

expectation *n.* 预料

22

Start with Yourself

—by Anonymous

When I was young and free and my imagination had no limits, I dreamed of changing the world. As I grew older and wiser, I discovered the world would not change, so I shortened my sights somewhat and decided to change only my country.

But, it too, seemed immovable.

从我做起
——佚名

在我年轻自由、想象力天马行空的时候，我曾梦想改变世界。随着我日渐成熟，日趋理智，我才发现世界不可能被改变，于是我降低标准，决定只去改变我的国家。

但我的国家似乎也无法改变。

As I grew into my *twilight* years, in one last *desperate* attempt, I *settled for* changing only my family, those closest to me, but alas, they would have none of it.

And now as I lie on my deathbed, I suddenly realize: If I had only changed myself first, then by example I would have changed my family.

From their *inspiration* and encouragement, I would then have been able to better my country and, who knows, I may have even changed the world.

当我进入迟暮之年，我想孤注一掷，决定只改变最亲近的家人，但是，哎！没有一个肯去改变。

而今，在我临终之际，我突然意识到：如果一开始我就改变自己，以自己为榜样，那么我就能依此来改变我的家人。

在他们的激励下，也许我就能让我的国家变得更加美好，谁知道呢，也许我连整个世界都可以改变呢！

---

twilight *n.* 黄昏
settle for 对……感到满足；满足于

desperate *adj.* 孤注一掷的
inspiration *n.* 激励

23

Stop Waiting

—by Anonymous

We *convince* ourselves that life will be better after we get married, have a baby, then another. Then we are *frustrated* that the kids aren't old enough and we'll be more content when they are. After that we're frustrated that we have teenagers to deal with. We will certainly be happy

莫在等
——佚名

我们总是认为等我们结了婚，生了孩子后，生活会更美满。可等有了孩子，我们又因为他们太小而惆怅，并认为等他们长大些懂事了，我们的生活更舒适。可随后等他们步入青春期，我们还要为应付他们的青春期问题而烦恼。心想等熬过这个非常时期，幸福就会大驾光临。我们常常自我安慰，等我们的另一半可以与我们同心协力，等我

---

convince v. 使相信

frustrate v. 使灰心的

when they are out of that stage. We tell ourselves that our life will be complete when our spouse gets his or her act together, when we get a nicer car, When we are able to go on a nice vacation, when we retire.

The truth is, there's no better time to be happy than right now.

Your life will always be filled with challenges. It's best to admit this to yourself and decide to be happy anyway. One of my favorite quotes comes from Alfred D Souza. He said, "For a long time it had seemed to me that life was about to begin—real life. But there was always some obstacle in the way, something to be gotten through first, some unfinished business, time still to be served, a debt to be paid. Then life would begin. At last it dawned on me that these obstacles were my life."

们坐拥更高档的轿车，等我们能够怡然度过一个惬意的假期，等我们退休之后，我们的人生就功德圆满了！

然而事实却是，没有比此时此刻更幸福的瞬间了。

生活总是充满挑战。你最好接受这一事实，毕竟无论如何都要选择快乐地生活。我最钟爱的名言中有一段摘自阿尔弗雷德·D·苏泽，他说："长期以来我都觉得真正的生活即将展开了，但一路走来，总是荆棘丛生，磕磕绊绊。例如有些事情得优先完成，还要预备出一些待定中的工作所要花费的时间，以及要去还清的债务。而后生活才会开始。最后我终于恍然大悟：这些障碍本身就是我的生活。"

This *perspective* has helped me to see that there is no way to happiness. Happiness is the way. So, treasure every moment that you have.

Stop waiting until you finish school, until you go back to school, until you lose ten pounds, until you gain ten pounds, until you have kids, until your kids leave the house, until you start work, until you retire, until you get married, until you get divorced, until Friday night, until Sunday morning, until you get a new car or home, until your car or home is paid off, until spring, until summer, until fall, until winter, until you are off welfare, until the first or fifteenth, until your song comes on, until you've had a drink, until you've *sobered up*, until you die, until you are born again to decide that there is no better time than right now to be happy.

这一观点让我意识到通往幸福的道路根本不存在。幸福本身就是一条路。因此，请珍惜你拥有的每一瞬间。

莫再等——莫等到你完成学业，或者重返校园继续深造；莫等你再瘦10磅，或者又增10磅；莫等你有了孩子，或者等孩子长大离家；莫等你开始工作，或者熬到退休；莫等你喜结连理，或者分道扬镳；莫等到星期五晚上，或者星期天清晨；莫等你买了新车或新房，还清车款或房款；莫等到春天，夏天，秋天，冬天；莫等你自食其力；莫等到第一次或第十五次；莫等你的主题歌响起；莫等你宿醉后或者清醒后；莫等到死亡逼近；莫等到你有幸再来世上走一遭，才明白，此时此刻才是你最应珍惜的幸福时光。

---

perspective *n.* 观点   sober up   酒醒

24

What Life Is All About

—by Anonymous

Life isn't about keeping score. It's not about how many friends you have, or how many people call you, or how accepted or unaccepted you are, not about if you have plans this weekend, or if you're alone. It isn't about who you're dating, who you used to date, how many people you've dated, or if you haven't been with

人生的意义
——佚名

人生不是一场记分赛，它不在于你拥有多少朋友，有多少人给你打电话，还是有多少人欢迎或排斥你；不在于这个周末你是有安排，还是独自度过；不在于你正在、曾经和谁约会，或与多少人约会过，或者从未与人约会；不在于你的家庭出身，或者你拥有多少财富，还

anyone at all. It isn't about who your family is or how much money they have, or what kind of car you drive, or where you're sent to school.

It's not about how beautiful or ugly you are, or what clothes you wear, what shoes you have on, or what kind of music you listen to. It's not about if your hair is *blonde*, red, black, brown, or green, or if your skin is too light or too dark.

It's not about what grades you get, how smart you are, how smart everyone else thinks you are, or how smart *standardized* tests say you are, or if this teacher likes you, or if this guy/girl likes you, or what clubs you're in, or how good you are at "your" sport. It's not about representing your whole being on a piece of paper and seeing who

是你开什么车，上什么学校。

人生不在于你长相的美丑；不在于你穿什么衣服，穿什么鞋，听什么音乐；不在于你的头发是金色、红色、黑色、褐色还是绿色；不在于你的皮肤是黑还是白。

人生不在于你得了多少分，你有多么聪明，或别人认为你有多么聪明，还是智力测试说明你有多么聪明；不在于这位老师是否喜欢你，这个男孩或女孩是否喜欢你；不在于你加入什么俱乐部，或你如何擅长某项运动；不在于你在一张试卷上的表现，况且谁会接受那个"书面的你"。

blonde *adj.* 金色的　　　　　　　standardized *adj.* 标准的

will "accept the written you".

But life is about whom you love and whom you hurt. It's about whom you make happy or unhappy purposefully. It's about keeping or betraying trust. It's about friendship, used as *sanctity*, or as a weapon. It's about what you say and mean, maybe hurtful, maybe heartening, about starting *rumors* and contributing to petty *gossip*. It's about what judgments you pass and why, and who your judgments are spread to.

But most of all, it's about using your life to touch or poison other people's hearts in such a way that could never occurred alone. Only you choose the way those hearts are affected and those choices are what life is all about.

然而，人生在于你爱谁和伤害了谁；在于你有意逗谁开心或惹谁生气；在于你是遵守诺言还是背信弃义；在于你是将友谊当作圣洁之物还是一种工具；在于你出口伤人还是让人耳沐春风；在于你是否散布谣言及捏造谈资；在于你做出的判断和如此判断的缘由，以及将你的判断向谁推广。

但最重要的是，人生在于你是用你的人生去感动他人的心灵还是无法避免地给他人造成伤害。如何影响这些心灵在于你的选择，那么这些选择就是你人生全部的意义。

---

sanctity　*n.*　圣洁；神圣　　　　　　　　　　rumor　*n.*　谣言
gossip　*n.*　小道传闻

25

True Nobility

— Ernest Hemingway

In a calm sea every man is a pilot. But all sunshine without shade, all pleasure without pain, is not life at all. Take the lot of the happiest—it is a *tangled yarn*. *Bereavements* and blessings, one following anther, make us sad and blessed by turns. Even death itself makes life more loving. Men come closest to their true selves in the *sober*

真正的高贵

—— 欧内斯特·海明威

在风平浪静的大海之上，每个人都是领航员。

但是只有晴空而没有阴霾，只有欢乐而没有痛苦的人生不是人生。以最幸福的人们为例——他们的人生就像一团纠结的纱线。丧亲之痛和声声祝福，此起彼伏，让我们悲喜交加。甚至死亡本身也使生命弥足珍

---

tangled   *adj.* 错综复杂的；纠缠的
bereavement   *n.* （亲人）丧亡

yarn   *n.* 纱；纱线
sober   *adj.* 严肃的；审慎的

moments of life, under the shadows of sorrow and loss.

In the affairs of life or of business, it is not intellect that tells so much as character, not brains so much as heart, not genius so much as self-control, patience, and discipline, regulated by judgment.

I have always believed that the man who has begun to live more seriously within begins to live more simply without. In an age of *extravagance* and waste, I wish I could show to the world how few the real wants of humanity are.

To regret one's errors *to the point* of not repeating them is true *repentance*. There is nothing noble in being superior to some other man. The true nobility is in being superior to your previous self.

贵。在人生的清醒时刻，在悲痛与失去的阴影之下，才最接近真实的自我。

在生活或事业中，与才智相比，性格更能指导我们；与头脑相比，心境更能引导我们；与天资相比，判断力所调控的自制力、耐心和行为准则更能让我们受益。

我一直相信，内心生活得严谨的人，他外在的生活也会因此而朴实无华。在这奢华浪费的年代，但愿我能向世人阐明，人类的真正需求少得多么可怜。

反思自己的错误，力求不再重蹈覆辙，这才是真正的悔悟。高人一等并不高贵。真正的高贵应是超越曾经的自己。

---

extravagance *n.* 奢侈　　　　　　　to the point 切题；中肯；简明扼要
repentance *n.* 忏悔；悔改

26

Think It Over

——by Anonymous

Today we have higher buildings and wider highways, but shorter *temperaments* and narrower points of view.

We spend more, but enjoy less. We have bigger houses, but smaller families. We have more compromises, but less time. We have more knowledge, but less judgement. We have more medicines, but less health.

好好想想
——佚名

今天我们拥有了更高层的楼阁以及更宽阔的公路，但是我们的性情却更为急躁，眼光也更加狭隘。

我们消耗掉得更多了，享受到的却变少了；我们拥有的住房更大，但家庭成员却变少了；我们妥协得更多，但个人时间却更少；我们拥有的知识更多了，可判断力却更差了；我们拥有的药品更多了，但健康状况却更不尽如人意了。

temperament *n.* 性格；秉性

We have multiplied our *possessions*, but reduced our values. We talk much, we love only a little, and we hate too much.

We reached the moon and came back, but we find it trouble some to cross our own street and meet our neighbors. We have conquered the outer space, but not our inner space.

We have higher income, but less morals. These are times with more liberty, but less joy. With much more food, but less nutrition.

These are days in which two salaries come home, but divorces increase. These are times of finer houses, but more broken homes.

That's why I propose that as of today — You do not keep anything for a special occasion, because every day that you live is a special

---

我们的财富与日倍增，但其价值却降低了；我们说得太多，却爱得太少，厌恶也随之变多了。

我们可以往返月球，却难以迈出一步去亲近左邻右舍；我们可以征服太空，却攻克不了内心。

我们的收入增加了，但道德却减少了；时代更加自由了，但快乐时光却短暂了；我们可以享用的食物越来越多，但所能摄取的营养却越来越少了。

现在，双收入家庭越来越多，但离婚率却大幅增长；住房越来越精致，但破碎的家庭却屡增不减。

所以我提议从今天开始——不要把东西预留到某一个特别时刻，因

---

possession *n.* 所有物

occasion. Search for knowledge, read more, sit on your front *porch* and admire the view without paying attention to the needs. Spend more time with your family, eat your favorite food, visit the place you love. Life is a chain of moments of enjoyment; not only about survival.

Use your crystal goblets. Do not save your best perfume... use it every time you feel you want it. Take out from your vocabulary phrases like, "one of these days" and "someday". Let's write that letter we thought of writing "one of these days"!

Let's tell our families and friends how much we love them. Never *pass up* a chance at adding laughter and joy to your life. Every day, hour, and minute are special; because you never know if it will be your last...

为你活的每一天都那么特别；学无止境，多读一些书，坐在家门前，享受眼前的美景，无欲无求；多花些时间和家人在一起，吃你爱吃的食物，去你想去的地方。生活是一串串的快乐时光；不仅仅是为了生存。

举起你的水晶高脚杯吧！不要吝惜你最好的香水，你想用的时候就享用吧！从你的字典里删去"有那么一天"或者"某一天"等词语；曾打算"有那么一天"要写的信，就在今天写了吧！

告诉我们的家人和朋友，我们是多么的爱他们。不要放过任何可以为你的生活带来欢笑与快乐的机会。每天、每时、每分钟都那么独特；因为你无从知道这是否将是你人生的最后一刻。

---

porch *n.* 门廊　　　　　　　　　　　pass up　放过；放弃；拒绝

27

Courage Is a Gift

— Gerri D Smith

Courage is daring to be Brave, *Enterprising*, *Bold*. In your business or personal life, how often do you question your thoughts, your action, or your motives? When you don't exercise the ability to always test yourself, you may lose not only your confidence, but more importantly, you lose the ability to focus, to know yourself, your friends, and your customers.

勇气是才能
——杰瑞·德·斯密斯

勇气是敢于冒险，勇于进取，勇往直前。在工作和生活中，你常常对自己的思想、行为或动机提出质疑吗？若你不经常锻炼并检验自己的能力，你不仅会丧失信心，更重要的是，你关注并认识自我、朋友和客户的能力也将消失殆尽。

enterprising *adj.* 有事业心的；有创新精神的   bold *adj.* 大胆的

When faced with decisions and challenges, asking yourself questions every day, every moment gives you the courage to discover what is important to you and what a particular situation means to you, and what result or solution you will like to accomplish.

Not many people experience life the way they want it to be. If things don't work out the way you want, don't find someone else to blame. Know what goals you want, then question your actions in reaching them. Compare your answers to what others may wish for you. After all, having a successful business or a life ot *contentment* requires you to know yourself and the goals that are best for you.

Courage is getting in the habit of inward and going with your highest feeling of what is true and what feels right for you. Apply this inner evaluation in your business and in your personal life. This is

---

面对抉择与挑战时，你要时刻警醒自己，这样你才有勇气去发现对自己至关重要的东西和对你有特殊意义的场景，以及你想实现的目标或解决方案。

很多人都过不上他们理想中的生活。如果现实与理想相距甚远，不要怨天尤人。要清楚你真正的目标，然后检验你追求目标所采取的行动，看其适当与否。把你的答案与别人对你寄予的期望加以比较。毕竟，成功的事业与幸福的家庭都需要你充分地认识自己，同时确立最佳目标。

勇气能让你形成自省的习惯，并让你的感受真实、恰当。假如你想成长起来并获得成功，把这种自我评价运用到工作和生活中，其内在价值极

---

contentment *n.* 满足；满意

important if you wish to grow and stay successful. It works!

Have the courage to be *curious*. A quest for knowledge about life and the people you interact with is good. Look for answers to helps. Over time, you can look back and discover the results of your actions (or reactions) to certain problems. Then when faced with future or similar problems, you'll have a ready solution.

Realize your weaknesses and work toward improving them. Continue to renew yourself and remember that life has a way of constantly testing your ability and courage to deal with it. When you can learn to appreciate the challenges in both your business and personal life, you find inner strength. Then you are able to bring about an inner peace and spirituality that gives you a good tool for building self-cofidence and self-esteem.

其重要。这确实有效！

　　勇于好奇。学习生活常识并了解与你打交道的人大有裨益。寻求答案来帮助你。过些时日，你可以回想在某些问题上，你曾经的行为（或反应）所产生的结果。这样，在面对未来或类似的问题时，你就会有的放矢。

　　认清自己的弱点并极力加以改进。要不断地给自己充电，并记住：生活总会不时地检验你处理问题的能力和勇气。当你懂得欣赏工作和生活中的挑战时，你就会发掘自身的潜能。而后，你将获得内心的安宁与精神的慰藉，这样会有助于你树立自信和建立自尊。

---

curious *adj.* 好奇的

There is something inside each of us that fuels our motivation, our passion, and our reason to succeed. Keep encouraging yourself to take the necessary risks to refuel your confidence. Question your motives. Then search for the answer. Question any doubts you or others may have about your courage to succeed. You are what is important.

Don't let negative thoughts get in the way of your progress and your goals. Control your thoughts. Think about what is important to you. When your thoughts are positive, they have a way of *replenishing* your courage. No matter how of ten unpleasant or difficult challenges get you down, don't give in to negative thinking. Just pick yourself up and move on. Focus on what gives you your strength and *uniqueness*.

每个人的内心都有一些东西可以激发我们的动机、激情和理智，以获取成功。想要信心倍增，就要不断地鼓舞自己冒一些必要的风险。审视自己的动机，然后寻求答案。倘若你有获得成功的勇气，不要轻信自己或他人对你的怀疑。你自己才是最重要的。

切不可让消极思想妨碍你的进步或实现你的目标。控制你的思想，想想什么对你最重要。积极的思想可帮你重整旗鼓。不论挑战多么频繁，多么艰难，多么令人沮丧，千万不要屈服于消极思想，要义无反顾地起身，继续前行，集中精力在那些给你力量和个性的事物上。

replenish *v.* 补充   uniqueness *n.* 独特性

Remember: motivation, passing, and your reason to succeed in life, as well as in business, are essential requirements to reaching your goals. Live life in a constant state of awareness, with peaceful thoughts, *a dash of* forcefulness, and a good measure of faith and spirituality. You will then be exercising your gift of courage.

谨记：无论是在生活，还是工作中，获取成功的动机、激情和理智，都是你实现目标不可或缺的条件。生活需要不断地思考，平静的思想，坚强的性格以及正确的信念和信仰，这样才能磨炼你的勇气。

---

a dash of 少许；一点儿

28

The Joy of Living

— A.T. Rowe

Joy in living comes from having fine emotions, trusting them, giving them the freedom of a bird in the open. Joy in living can never be *assumed* as a pose, or put on from the outside as a mask. People who have this joy do not need to talk about it; they *radiate* it. They just live out their joy and let it *splash* its sunlight and glow into other lives as naturally as bird sings.

生活的乐趣
——A.T.罗

生活之乐趣源于美妙充沛的情感，并对其深信不疑，任由它们如同鸟儿高翔于天空般地自由自在。生活之乐趣无法靠搔首弄姿惺惺作态而表露于外，也无法凭借戴上一张面具来伪装得深藏不露。拥有生活乐趣的人们无须高谈阔论，自然就会散发快乐的气息。他们沉浸在自己的快乐之中，也自然而然地将这样的快乐传播给他人，犹如是鸟儿就必将歌唱一样。

assumed *adj.* 假装的

radiate *v.* 射出；散发

splash *v.* 使(液体)溅起；(指液体)溅落

We can never get it by working for it directly. It comes, like happiness, to those who are *aiming* at something higher. It is a by product of great, simple living. The joy of living comes from what we put into living, not from what we seek to get from it.

　　直接追求生活的乐趣，只会使乐趣渐行渐远。它与幸福一样，都青睐那些高瞻远瞩的人们。高雅、简单的生活本身就孕育着乐趣。生活之乐趣源于我们对生活的投入，而非刻意地追寻。

---

aim　*v.* 瞄准

The Life I Desired

——William Somerset Maugham

That must be the story of innumerable couples, and the pattern of life it offers has a homely grace. It reminds you of a *placid rivulet*, meandering smoothly through green *pastures* and shaded by pleasant trees, till at last it falls into the vasty sea; but the sea is so calm, so silent, so indifferent, that you are troubled

我所追求的生活

——威廉·萨姆塞特·毛姆

这一定是世上无数对夫妻的生活写照，这种生活模式体现了一种天伦之美。它使人想起一条平静的溪流，蜿蜒畅游过绿茵草场，被大树的浓荫所遮蔽，最后注入烟波浩渺的大海；但是大海如此平静，如此沉默，如此不动声色，你会突然感到莫名的不安。也许这只是我

placid *adj.* 温和的   rivulet *n.* 小河；小溪
pasture *n.* 牧草地；牧场

suddenly by a vague uneasiness. Perhaps it is only by a kink in my nature, strong in me even in those days, that I felt in such an existence, the share of the great majority, something *amiss*. I recognized its social value. I saw its ordered happiness, but a fever in my blood asked for a wilder course. There seemed to me something alarming in such easy delights. In my heart was desire to live more dangerously. I was not unprepared for jagged rocks and treacherous, shoals it I could only have change — change and the excitement of *unforeseen*.

自己的一种荒诞想法，在那样的时代，这想法对我影响很深：我认为像大多数人一样的生活，似乎欠缺了点儿什么。我承认这种生活有社会价值，我也看到了它那井然有序的幸福，但我血液里的热情却渴望一种更狂野的旅程。这样的安逸中好像有一种令我惊慌的东西。我的心渴望一种更加惊险刺激的生活。只要生活中还有变迁——以及不可知的刺激，我愿意踏上怪石嶙峋的山崖，奔赴暗礁遍布的海滩。

---

amiss *adj.* 不妥的　　　　　　　　unforeseen *adj.* 始料不及的

Duty, Honor, Country

— MacArthur

The shadows are lengthening for me. The twilight is here. My days of old have vanished, tone and tint. They have gone *glimmering* through the dreams of things that were. Their memory is one of wondrous beauty, watered by tears, and *coaxed* and *caressed* by the smiles of yesterday. I listen vainly,

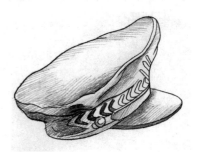

责任、荣誉、国家
　　——麦克阿瑟

我的生命已近黄昏，暮色已经降临，我昔日的风采和荣誉已消失殆尽。它们随着对昔日成就的憧憬，伴着落日的余晖一同消失。精妙绝伦的美丽，经泪水洗涤过的双眸和昨日笑意盈盈的安慰和爱抚后，构成了昔日的美好记忆。我渴望但徒然地倾听那微弱而迷人的起床号

---

glimmering *adj.* 微弱地发光的　　　　　　　coax *v.* 安慰；哄
caress *v.* 爱抚

MCGRAW-HILL

but with thirsty ears, for the *witching* melody of faint *bugles* blowing reveille, of far drums beating the long roll. In my dreams I hear again the crash of guns, the rattle of *musketry*, the strange, mournful *mutter* of the battlefield.

But in the evening of my memory, always I come back to West Point. Always there echoes and re-echoes: Duty, Honor, Country. Today marks my final roll call with you, but I want you to know that when I cross the river my last conscious thoughts will be of The Corps, and The Corps, and The Corps.

声，咚咚作响的军鼓声。我在梦幻中依稀又听到了隆隆的炮声，滑膛枪的鸣放声，战场上那古怪而又悲伤的呻吟声。

然而，暮年的回忆经常将我带回西点军校。耳边始终回响着：责任，荣誉，国家。今天是我对你们进行最后一次点名。但我希望你们知道，当我死去时，我最后想到的一定是海军陆战队，海军陆战队，还是海军陆战队。

---

witching *adj.* 有魅力的
musketry *n.* 步枪射击

bugle *n.* 喇叭；军号
mutter *n.* 咕哝

31

The Road to Success

— Andrew Carnegie

It is well that young men should begin at the beginning and occupy the most *subordinate* positions. Many of the leading businessmen of Pittsburgh had a serious responsibility *thrust upon* them at the very *threshold* of their career. They were introduced to the broom, and spent the first hours of their business lives sweeping out the office. I notice

成功之道
——安德鲁·卡耐基

年轻人在创业之初从最底层干起是件好事。匹兹堡的很多商业巨贾，在他们创业之初，都曾肩负此"重任"。在事业生涯的最初期，他们曾与扫帚为舞，打扫办公室。我注意到现在的办公室都有清洁

subordinate *adj.* 从属的；下级的　　　　thrust upon　迫使……接受
threshold　*n.*　门槛

we have *janitors* and janitresses now in offices, and our young men unfortunately miss that *salutary* branch of business education. But if by chance the professional sweeper is absent any morning, the boy who has the genius of the future partner in him will not *hesitate* to try his hand at the broom. It does not hurt the newest comer to sweep out the office if necessary. I was one of those sweepers myself.

Assuming that you have all *obtained* employment and are fairly started, my advice to you is "aim high". I would not give a fig for the young man who does not already see himself the partner or the head of an important firm. Do not rest content for a moment in your thoughts as head clerk, or foreman, or general manager in any concern, no matter how extensive. Say to yourself, "My place is at the top." Be king in your dreams.

工，于是年轻人很不幸地错过了事业教育中这个有益的环节。不过，如果哪天上午碰巧清洁工没有来，某个具有未来合伙人气质的年轻人会毫不犹豫地拿起扫帚。必要时新来的员工扫扫地也无妨，并不会因此而损失什么。我曾经也扫过地。

假如你已被录用，并且有了一个良好的开端，我的建议是：要志存高远。对于那些尚未把自己想象成是一家大公司未来的老板或者是合伙人的年轻人，我会不屑一顾。不论职位有多高，你的内心都不要满足于做一个总管，领班或者总经理。要对自己说：我要迈向顶尖！要梦寐以求登峰造极！

---

janitor *n.* 看管房屋的人
hesitate *v.* 不情愿；犹豫

salutary *adj.* 有益的
obtain *v.* 获得；得到

And here is the prime condition of success, the great secret: concentrate your energy, thought, and capital *exclusively* upon the business in which you are engaged. Having begun in one line, resolve to fight it out on that line, to lead in it, adopt every improvement, have the best machinery, and know the most about it.

The concerns which fail are those which have *scattered* their capital, which means that they have scattered their brains also. They have investments in this, or that, or the other, here there, and everywhere. "Don't put all your eggs in one basket." is all wrong. I tell you to "put all your eggs in one basket, and then watch that basket." Look round you and take notice, men who do that not often fail. It is easy to watch and carry the one basket. It is trying to carry

---

　　成功的首要条件和最大秘诀就是：把你的精力、见解和资本全部投入在你正从事的事业上。一旦开始从事某种职业，就要下定决心在那片领域内闯出一片天地来，做这一行的领军人物，采纳意见并改进，使用最优良的装备，对专业知识熟稔于心。

　　一些公司失败的原因就在于他们分散了资金，因为分散资金意味着分散他们的精力。他们这也投资，那也投资。"不要把所有的鸡蛋放在一个篮子里"的说法大错特错。我的观点是："把所有的鸡蛋都放在一个篮子里，然后小心地看好那个篮子。"看看你周围，你会注意到：这么做的人其实很少失败。看管和携带一个篮子并不难。在这个国家，人们总是试图

---

exclusively *adv.* 专门地　　　　　　　　　　scatter *v.* 散开；散布；散播

too many baskets that breaks most eggs in this country. He who carries three baskets must put one on his head, which is apt to *tumble* and trip him up. One fault of the American businessman is lack of concentration.

To summarise what I have said: aim for the highest; never enter a bar room; do not touch liquor, or if at all only at meals; never speculate; never *indorse* be yond your surplus cash fund; make the firm's interest yours; break orders always to save owners; concentrate; put all your eggs in one basket, and watch that basket; *expenditure* always within *revenue*; lastly, be not impatient, for as Emerson says, "no one can cheat you out of ultimate success but yourselves."

提很多篮子，所以才会打破大部分鸡蛋。提三个篮子的人，必须要把一个顶在头上，而这个篮子很可能会掉下来，把自己绊倒。美国商人的一个缺点就是不够专注。

我的话归纳如下：要志存高远；不要出入酒吧；要滴酒不沾，或仅在用餐时喝少许；不要投机；不要寅吃卯粮；要把公司的利益当作自己的利益；取消订货的目的永远是为了挽留货主；要专注；要把所有的鸡蛋放在一个篮子里，然后小心地看好它；要量入为出；最后，要有耐心，正如爱默生所言，"谁都无法阻止你最终成功，除非你自己承认自己失败。"

---

tumble *v.* 翻滚
expenditure *n.* (尤指金钱的)支出额

indorse *v.* 认可
revenue *n.* 收入；收益

32

Youth

— Samual Ullman

Youth is not a time of life, it is a state of mind; it is not a matter of *rosy* cheeks, red lips and supple knees, it is a matter of the will, a quality of the imagination, a vigor of the emotions: it is the freshness of the deep springs of life.

Youth means a temperamental *predominance* of courage over timidity, of

---

青春

——塞缪尔·厄尔曼

青春不是年华，而是心境；青春不是桃面、丹唇、柔膝，而是深沉的意志，恢宏的想象，炙热的情感；青春是生命的深泉在涌流。

青春气贯长虹，勇锐盖过怯弱，进取压倒苟安。如此锐气，二十后

---

rosy *adj.* （脸颊）红润的   predominance *n.* 优势

the *appetite* for adventure over the love of ease. This often exists in a man of 60 more than a boy of 20. Nobody grows old merely by a number of years. We grow old by deserting our ideals.

Years may wrinkle the skin, but to give up enthusiasm wrinkles the soul. Worry, fear, *self-distrust* bows the heart and turns the spirit back to dust.

Whether 60 or 16, there is in every human being's heart the lure of wonders, the unfailing childlike appetite for what's next and the joy of the game of living. In the center of your heart and my heart there's a *wireless* station: so long as it receives messages of beauty, hope, cheer, courage and power from men and from the infinite, so long as you are young.

When the *aerials* are down, and your spirit is covered with snows of cynicism and the ice of pessimism, then you've grown old, even at 20, but as long as your aerials are up, to catch waves of optimism, there is hope you may die young at 80.

生而有之，六旬男子则更多见。年岁有加，并非垂老；理想丢弃，方堕暮年。

岁月悠悠，衰微只及肌肤；热忱抛却，颓废必致灵魂。忧烦，惶恐，丧失自信，定使心灵扭曲，意气如灰。

无论年届花甲，拟或二八芳龄，心中皆有生命之欢乐，奇迹之诱惑，孩童般天真久盛不衰。人人心中皆有一台天线，只要你从天上人间接受美好、希望、欢乐、勇气和力量的信号，你就青春永驻，风华常存。

一旦天线倒塌，锐气便被冰雪覆盖，玩世不恭、自暴自弃油然而生，即使年方二十，实已垂垂老矣；然则只要树起天线，捕捉乐观信号，你就有望在八十高龄告别尘寰时仍觉年轻。

---

appetite *n.* 强烈欲望
wireless *n.* 无线电

self-distrust *n.* 没有信心
aerial *n.* 天线

33

If I Rest, I Rust

— Orison Marden

The significant inscription found on an old key —"If I rest, I rust." —would be an excellent motto for those who are afflicted with slightest bit of *idleness*. Even the most industrious person might adopt it with advantage to serve as a reminder that, if one allows his faculties to rest, like the iron in the unused key, they will soon show signs of

如果我休息，我就会生锈
——奥里森·马登

在一把旧钥匙上发现了一则意义深远的铭文——如果我休息，我就会生锈。对于那些懒散而烦恼的人来说，这将是至理名言。甚至最为勤勉的人也以此作为警示：如果一个人有才能而不用，就像废弃钥匙上的铁一样，这些才能就会很快生锈，并最终无法完成安排给自己的工作。

idleness *n.* 懒惰

rust and, ultimately, cannot do the work required of them.

Those who would *attain* the heights reached and kept by great men must keep their faculties polished by constant use, so that they may unlock the doors of knowledge, the gates that guard entrances to the professions, to science, art, literature, agriculture — every department of human endeavor.

Industry keeps bright the key that opens the treasury of achievement. If Hugh Miller, after toiling all day in quarry, had devoted his evenings to rest and recreation, he would never have become a famous geologist. The celebrated *mathematician*, Edmund

---

有些人想取得伟人所获得并保持的成就，他们就必须不断运用自身才能，以便开启知识的大门，即那些通往人类努力探求的各个领域的大门，这些领域包括各种职业：科学、艺术、文学、农业等。

勤奋使开启成功宝库的钥匙保持光亮。如果休·米勒在采石场劳作一天后，晚上的时光用来休息消遣的话，他就不会成为名垂青史的地质学家。著名数学家爱德蒙·斯通如果闲暇时无所事事，就不会出版数学词

---

attain *v.* 获得   mathematician *n.* 数学家

Stone would never have published a mathematical dictionary, never have found the key to science of mathematics, if he had given his spare moments to idleness. Had the little Scotch lad, Ferguson, had allowed the busy brain to go to sleep while he tended sheep on the hillside, instead of calculating the position of the stars by a string of beads, he would never become a famous *astronomer*.

Labor vanquishes all—not inconstant, spasmodic or ill-directed labor; but faithful, unremitting, daily effort toward a well-directed purpose. Just as truly as eternal vigilance is the price of liberty, so is *eternal* industry the price of noble and enduring success.

典，也不会发现开启数学之门的钥匙。如果苏格兰青年弗格森在山坡上放羊时，让他那思维活跃的大脑处于休息状态，而不是借助一串珠子计算星星的位置，他就不会成为著名的天文学家。

　　劳动征服一切。这里所指的劳动不是断断续续的，间歇性的或方向偏差的劳动，而是坚定的，不懈的，方向正确的每日劳动。正如要想拥有自由就要时刻保持警惕一样，要想取得伟大的、持久的成功，就必须坚持不懈地努力。

---

astronomer　n.　天文学家　　　　　　　　　　eternal　adj.　永久的

34

Ambition

— Joseph Epstein

t is not difficult to imagine a world short of ambition. It would probably be a kinder world: without demands, without *abrasions*, without disappointments. People would have time for reflection. Such work as they did would not be for themselves but for the collectivity. Competition would never enter in. Conflict would be eliminated, tension become

抱负

——约瑟夫·艾普斯坦

　　个缺乏抱负的世界将会怎样，这不难想象。或许，这将是一个更为友善的世界：没有渴求，没有摩擦，没有失望。人们将有时间进行反思。他们所从事的工作将不是为了他们自身，而是为了整个集体。竞争永远不会介入；冲突将被消除。人们的紧张关系将成为过往云

---

abrasion *n.* 摩擦

a thing of the past. The stress of creation would be at an end. Art would no longer be troubling, but purely celebratory in its functions. Longevity would be increased, for fewer people would die of heart attack or stroke caused by *tumultuous* endeavor. Anxiety would be extinct. Time would stretch on and on, with ambition long departed from the human heart. Ah, how unrelievedly boring life would be?

There is a strong view that holds that success is a myth, and ambition therefore a sham. Does this mean that success does not really exist? That achievement is at bottom empty? That efforts of men and women are of no significance alongside the force of movements and events? Now not all success, obviously, is worth esteeming, nor all *ambition* worth cultivating. Which are and which are not is something one soon enough learns on one's own. But

---

烟。创造的重压将得以终结。艺术将不再惹人费神，其功能将纯粹为了庆典。人的寿命将会更长，因为由激烈拼争引起的心脏病和中风所导致的死亡将越来越少。焦虑将会消失。时光流逝，抱负却早已远离人心。啊，长此以往人生将变得多么乏味无聊！

有一种盛行的观点认为，成功是一种神话，因此抱负亦属虚幻。这是不是说实际上并不存在成功？成就本身就是一场空？与诸多运动和事件的力量相比，男男女女的努力显得微不足？显然，并非所有的成功都值得景仰，也并非所有的抱负都值得追求。对值得和不值得的选择，一个人自然

---

tumultuous *adj.* 热烈的　　　　　　　　ambition *n.* 抱负；梦想

even the most cynical secretly admit that success exists; that achievement counts for a great deal; and that the true myth is that the actions of men and women are useless. To believe otherwise is to take on a point of view that is likely to deranging. It is, in its implications, to remove all motives for competence, in attainment, and regard for posterity.

We do not choose to be born. We do not choose our parents. We do not choose our historical *epoch*, the country of our birth, or the *immediate* circumstances of our upbringing. We do not, most of us, choose to die; nor do we choose the time or conditions of our death. But within all this realm of choicelessness, we do choose how we

---

而然很快就能学会。但即使是最为愤世嫉俗的人暗地里也承认，成功确实存在，成就的意义举足轻重，而把世上男男女女的所作所为说成是徒劳无功才是真正的无稽之谈。认为成功不存在的观点很可能造成混乱。这种观点的本意是一笔勾销所有提高能力的动机，求取业绩的兴趣和对子孙后代的关注。

我们无法选择出生，无法选择父母，无法选择出生的历史时期与国家，或是成长的周遭环境。我们大多数人都无法选择死亡，无法选择死亡的时间或条件。但是在这些无法选择之中，我们的确可以选择自己的生活

---

epoch *n.* 时期；纪元　　　　　　　　　　　immediate *adj.* 临近的

shall live: courageously or in cowardice, *honorably* or dishonorably, with purpose or in drift. We decide what is important and what is trivial in life. We decide that what makes us significant is either what we do or what we refuse to do. But no matter how indifferent the universe to our choices and decisions, these choices and decisions are ours to make. We decide. We choose. And as we decide and choose, so are our lives formed. In the end, forming our own *destiny* is what ambition about.

方式：是勇敢无畏还是胆小怯懦，是光明磊落还是厚颜无耻，是目标坚定还是随波逐流。我们决定生活中哪些至关重要，哪些微不足道。我们决定，用以显示我们自身重要性的，不是我们做了什么，就是我们拒绝做些什么。但是不论世界对我们所做的选择和决定有多么漠不关心，这些选择和决定终究是我们自己做出的。我们决定，我们选择。而当我们决定和选择时，我们的生活便得以形成。最终构筑我们命运的就是抱负之所在。

honorably *adv.* 光荣地；体面地　　　　　　　　destiny *n.* 命运

When Love Reckons You

— Kahlil Gibran

When love *beckons* to you, follow him, though his ways are hard and steep. And when his wings enfold you, yield to him, though the sword hidden among his pinions may wound you. And when he speaks to you, believe in him, though his voice may shatter your dreams as the north wind lays waste the garden.

爱的召唤

——卡利尔·纪伯伦

当爱召唤你时，请追随她，尽管爱的道路艰难险峻。当爱的羽翼拥抱你时，请顺从她，尽管隐藏在其羽翼之下的剑可能会伤到你。当爱向你诉说时，请相信她，尽管她的声音可能打破你的梦想，就如同北风吹落花园里所有的花瓣。

beckon *v.* 召唤

For even as love crowns you so shall he crucify you. Even as he is for your growth so is he for your pruning. Even as he *ascends* to your height and caresses your tenderest branches that quiver in the sun, so shall he descend to your roots and shake them in their *clinging to* the earth.

But if, in your fear, you would seek only love's peace and love's pleasure, then it is better for you that you cover your nakedness and pass out of love's threshing-floor, into the seasonless world where you shall laugh, but not all of your laughter, and weep, not all of your tears. Love gives naught but itself takes naught but from itself. Love possesses not, nor would it be possessed, for love is sufficient unto love.

Love has no other desire but to fulfill itself. But if you love and must have desires, let these be your desires:

爱会给你戴上桂冠，也会折磨你。爱会助你成长，也会给你修枝。爱会上升到枝头，爱抚你在阳光下颤动力的嫩枝，也会下潜至根部，撼动你紧抓泥土的根基。

但是，如果你在恐惧之中只想寻求爱的平和与快乐，那你就最好掩盖真实的自我，避开爱的考验，进入不分季节的世界，在那里你将欢笑，但并非开怀大笑，你将哭泣，但并非尽情地哭。爱只将自己付出，也只得到自己。爱一无所有，也不会为谁所有，因为爱本身就已自足。

爱除了实现自我别无他求。但是如果你爱而又不得不有所求，那就请期望：

---

ascend *v.* 上升   cling to   紧抓

To melt and be like a running brook that sings its *melody* to the night.

To know the pain of too much tenderness.

To be wounded by your understanding of love.

And to bleed willingly and joyfully.

To wake at dawn with a winged heart and give thanks for another day of loving;

To rest at the noon hour and *meditate* love's *ecstasy*;

To return home at eventide with gratitude;

And then to sleep with a prayer for the beloved in your heart and a song of praise upon you lips.

将自己融化并像奔流的溪水一般向夜晚吟唱自己优美的曲调。

明了过多的温柔所带来的苦痛。

被自己对爱的理解所伤害；

并情愿快乐地悲伤。

在黎明带着轻快的心醒来并感谢又一个有家的日子；

在黄昏怀着感恩之心回家；

然后为内心所爱之人祈祷，吟唱赞美之歌，并带着祷告和歌声入眠。

---

melody *n.* 曲调　　　　　　　　　　　meditate *v.* 冥想；深思
ecstasy *n.* 狂喜

36

Be Happy!

— John Masefield

"The days that make us happy make us wise."

— John Masefield

When I first read this line by England's Poet Laureate, it startled me. What did Masefield mean? Without thinking about it much, I had always assumed that the opposite was true. But his sober assurance was arresting. I could not forget it.

快乐起来
——约翰·梅斯菲尔德

"快乐的日子使人睿智。"——约翰·梅斯菲尔德
　　第一次读到英国桂冠诗人梅斯菲尔德的这行诗时，我感到十分震惊。他想表达什么意思？我以前从未对此仔细考虑，总是认定这行诗反过来才正确。但他冷静而又胸有成竹的表达引起了我的注意，令我无法忘怀。

Finally, I seemed to *grasp* his meaning and realized that here was a *profound* observation. The wisdom that happiness makes possible lies in clear perception, not fogged by anxiety nor dimmed by despair and *boredom*, and without the blind spots caused by fear.

Active happiness—not mere satisfaction or contentment —often comes suddenly, like an April shower or the unfolding of a bud. Then you discover what kind of wisdom has accompanied it. The grass is greener; bird songs are sweeter; the shortcomings of your friends are more understandable and more forgivable. Happiness is like a pair of eyeglasses correcting your spiritual vision.

Nor are the insights of happiness limited to what is near around you. Unhappy, with your thoughts turned in upon your emotional

---

终于，我似乎领会了他的意思，并意识到这行诗意义深远。快乐带来的睿智存在于敏锐的洞察力之间，不会因忧虑而含混迷惑，也不会因绝望和厌倦而黯然模糊，更不会因恐惧而造成盲点。

积极的快乐——并非单纯的满意或知足——通常不期而至，就像四月里突然下起的春雨，或是花蕾的突然绽放。然后，你就会发觉与快乐结伴而来的究竟是何种智慧。草地更为青翠，鸟吟更为甜美，朋友的缺点也变得更能让人理解，宽容。快乐就像是一副眼镜，可以矫正你的精神视力。

快乐的视野并不仅限于你周围的事物。当你不快乐时，你的思维陷入情感上的悲哀，你的眼界就像是被一道墙给阻隔了，而当你快乐时，这道

---

grasp *v.* 领悟
boredom *n.* 厌倦

profound *adj.* 深刻的

101

woes, your vision is cut short as though by a wall. Happy, the wall *crumbles*.

The long vista is there for the seeing. The ground at your feet, the world about you—people, thoughts, emotions, pressures—are now *fitted into* the larger scene. Everything assumes a fairer proportion. And here is the beginning of wisdom.

墙就会砰然倒塌。

你的眼界变得更为宽广。你脚下的大地，你身边的世界，包括人，思想，情感和压力，现在都融入了更为广阔的景象之中，其间每件事物的比例都更加合理。而这就是睿智的起始。

---

crumble *v.* 坍塌   fit into   与……融为一体

37.

The Love of Beauty
— by Anonymous

The love of beauty is an essential part of all healthy human nature. It is a moral quality. The absence of it is not an assured ground of *condemnation*, but the presence of it is an invariable sign of goodness of heart. In proportion to the degree in which it is felt will probably be the degree in which nobleness and beauty of character will be attained.

爱美
——佚名

爱美是整个健全人性不可或缺之一部分。它是一种道德品质。缺乏这种品质并不能作为受到责难的充分理由，但是拥有这种品质则是心灵美好的永恒标志。品德的高尚与美好所达到的程度可能与对美的感受程度成正比。

condemnation *n.* 指责；谴责

Natural beauty is an *all-pervading* presence. The universe is its temple. It unfolds into the numberless flowers of spring. It waves in the branches of trees and the green blades of grass. It haunts the depths of the earth and the sea. It gleams from the hues of the shell and the precious stone. And not only these minute objects but the oceans, the mountains, the clouds, the stars, the rising and the setting sun—all overflow with beauty. This beauty is so precious, and so congenial to our tenderest and noblest feelings, that it is painful to think of the multitude of people living in the midst of it and yet remaining almost blind to it.

All persons should seek to become acquainted with the beauty in nature. There is not a worm we tread upon, nor a leaf that dances *merrily* as it falls before the autumn winds, but calls for our study and

大自然的美无处不在，整个宇宙就是美的殿堂。美，在春日百花中绽放；美，在绿叶嫩枝间摇曳；美，在深海幽谷里游弋；美，在奇石与贝壳的缤纷色彩中闪烁。不只是这些细微之物，还有海洋、山川、云彩、繁星、日升日落 —— 一切都洋溢着美。这样的美是如此珍贵，与我们最温柔，最高尚的情愫是如此相宜。然而，想到很多人置身于美之中，却几乎对它熟视无睹，真是令人痛心不已。

所有的人都应该去认识大自然之美。没有一条我们踩过的小虫，没有一片在秋风拂掠之际飞舞的树叶不值得我们研究与赞赏。欣赏美的能力不

all-pervading *adj.* 普及的；普遍的　　　　　merrily *adv* 轻快地

admiration. The power to appreciated beauty not merely increases our sources of happiness—it *enlarges* our moral nature, too. Beauty calms our restlessness and dispels our cares. Go into the fields or the woods, spend a summer day by the sea or the mountains, and all your little *perplexities* and anxieties will vanish. Listen to sweet music, and your foolish fears and petty jealousies will pass away. The beauty of the world helps us to seek and find the beauty of goodness.

仅增加了我们快乐的来源，也加强了我们德行的修养。美使我们不安的心平静下来，也驱散了我们的忧虑。到田野或森林去，在夏日的海边或山上待上一天，那么你所有微不足道的困惑与焦虑都会烟消云散。倾听悦耳的音乐，你那愚蠢的恐惧与狭隘的嫉妒都会过去。世界之美将有助于我们找到为善之美。

---

enlarge *v.* 扩大；进一步补充   perplexity *n.* 困惑

38

Relish the Moment

— by Anonymous

Tucked away in our *subconsciousness* is an idyllic vision. We see ourselves on a long trip that spans the moment. We are traveling by train. Out the windows, we drink in the passing scene of cars on nearby highways, of children waving at a crossing, of cattle grazing on a distant hillside, of smoke pouring from a power plant, of row upon

品味现在
　　——佚名

　　我们的潜意识里藏着一派田园诗般的风光！我们仿佛身处一次横贯大陆的漫漫旅程之中！乘着火车，我们领略着窗外流动的景色：附近高速公路上奔驰的汽车、十字路口处招手的孩童、远山上吃草的牛群、源源不断地从电厂排放出的烟尘、一片片的玉米和小麦、平原与山

subconsciousness　*n*　潜意识

row of corn ad wheat, of *flatlands* and valleys, of mountains and rolling hillsides, of city skylines and village halls.

But uppermost in our minds is the final destination. On a certain day at a certain hour, we will pull into the station. Bands will be playing and flags waving. Once we get there, so many wonderful dreams will come true and the pieces of our lives will fit together like a completed *jigsaw* puzzle. How restlessly we pace the aisles, damning the minutes for loitering—waiting, waiting, waiting for the station.

"When we reach the station, that will be it!" we cry. "When I'm 18." "When I buy a new 450SL Mercedes Benz!" "When I put the last kid through college." "When I have paid off the *mortgage*!" "When I get a promotion." "When I reach the age of retirement, I shall live happily ever after!"

谷、群山与绵延的丘陵、天空映衬下城市的轮廓，以及乡间的庄园宅第！

然而我们心里想得最多的却是最终的目的地！在某一天的某一时刻，我们将会抵达进站！迎接我们的将是乐队和飘舞的彩旗～一旦到了那儿，多少美梦将成为现实，我们的生活也将变得完整，如同一块理好了的拼图！可是我们现在在过道里不耐烦地踱来踱去，咒骂火车的拖拖拉拉！我们期待着，期待着，期待着火车进站的那一刻！

"当我们到站的时候，一切就都好了！"我们呼喊着。"当我18岁的时候！""当我有了一辆新450SL奔驰的时候！""当我供最小的孩子念完大学的时候！""当我偿清贷款的时候！""当我官升高任的时候！""当我到了退休的时候，就可以从此过上幸福的生活啦！"

flatland *n.* 平原
mortgage *n.* 抵押贷款

jigsaw *n.* 拼图

Sooner or later, we must realize there is no station, no one place to arrive at once and for all. The true joy of life is the trip. The station is only a dream. It *constantly* outdistances us.

It isn't the burdens of today that drive men mad. It is the regrets over yesterday and the fear of tomorrow. Regret and fear are twin thieves who rob us of today.

So stop pacing the aisles and counting the miles. Instead, climb more mountains, eat more ice cream, go barefoot more often, swim more rivers, watch more sunsets, laugh more, cry less. Life must be lived as we go along. The station will come soon enough.

　　可是我们终究会认识到人生的旅途中并没有车站，也没有能够"一劳永逸"的地方！生活的真正乐趣在于旅行的过程，而车站不过是个梦，它始终遥遥领先于我们！

　　真正令人发疯的不是今日的负担，而是对昨日的悔恨及对明日的恐惧！悔恨与恐惧是一对孪生窃贼，将今天从你我身边偷走！

　　那么就不要在过道里徘徊吧，别老惦记着你离车站还有多远！何不换一种活法，将更多的高山攀爬，多吃点儿冰淇淋甜甜嘴巴，经常光着脚板儿溜达，在更多的河流里畅游，多看看夕阳西下，多点欢笑哈哈，少让泪水滴答！生活得一边过一边瞧！车站就会很快到达！

---

constantly　adv.　不变地；一直存在地

The Happy Door

— by Anonymous

Happiness is like a *pebble dropped into* a pool to set in motion an ever-widening circle of ripples. As Stevenson has said, being happy is a duty.

There is no exact definition of the word happiness. Happy people are happy for all sorts of reasons. The key is not wealth or physical well-being, since we find beggars,

---

快乐之门
—— 佚名

快乐就像一块为了激起阵阵涟漪而丢进池塘的小石头。正好史蒂文森所说，快乐是一种责任。

快乐这个词并没有确切的定义，快乐的人快乐的理由多种多样。快乐的关键并不是财富或身体健康，因为我们发现有些乞丐，残疾人和所谓的

---

pebble *n.* 砾石

drop into 把……丢进

invalids and so-called failures, who are extremely happy.

Being happy is a sort of unexpected dividend. But staying happy is an accomplishment, a triumph of soul and character. It is not selfish to strive for it. It is, indeed, a duty to ourselves and others.

Being unhappy is like an *infectious* disease. It causes people to shrink away from the sufferer. He soon finds himself alone, *miserable* and embittered. There is, however, a cure so simple as to seem, at first glance, ridiculous; if you don't feel happy, pretend to be!

It works. Before long you will find that instead of repelling people, you attract them. You discover how deeply rewarding it is to be the center of wider and wider circles of good will.

失败者也都非常快乐。

　　快乐是一种意外的收获，但保持快乐却是一种成就，一种灵性的胜利。努力追寻快乐并不自私，实际上，这是我们对自己和他人应尽的责任。

　　不快乐就像传染病，它使得人们都躲避不快乐的人。不快乐的人很快就会发现自己处于孤独、悲惨、痛苦的境地。然而，有一种简单得看似荒谬的治病良方：如果你不快乐，就假装你很快乐！

　　这很有效。不久你就会发现，别人不再躲着你了，相反，你开始吸引别人了。你会发觉，做一块能激起好意涟漪的小石头有多么值得。

---

infectious *adj* 传染的　　　　　　　　miserable *adj.* 痛苦的

Then the make-believe becomes a reality. You possess the secret of peace of mind, and can forget yourself in being of service to others.

Being happy, once it is realized as a duty and established as a habit, opens doors into unimaginable gardens *thronged* with grateful friends.

然后假装就变成了现实。你拥有了使心灵平静的秘密，会因帮助他人而忘我。

一旦你认识到快乐是一种责任并使快乐成为习惯，通向不可思议的乐园的大门就会向你敞开，那里满是感激你的朋友。

throng *v.* 涌向；蜂拥

40

Born to Win

— by Anonymous

Each human being is born as something new, something that never existed before. Each is born with the capacity to win at life. Each person has a unique way of seeing, hearing, touching, tasting and thinking. Each has his or her own unique potentials—*capabilities* and limitations. Each can be a significant,

生而为赢
——佚名

人皆生而为赢,为前所未有之存在;人皆生而为赢。人皆有其特立独行之方式去审视、聆听、触摸、品位及思考,因而都具备独特潜质——能力和局限。人皆能举足轻重,思虑明达,洞察秋毫,富有创意,成就功业。

---

capability *n* 能力

thinking, aware, and creative being—a productive person, a winner.

The word "winner" and "loser" have many meanings. When we refer to a person as a winner, we do not mean one who makes someone else lose. To us, a winner is one who responds *authentically* by being credible, *trustworthy*, responsive, and genuine, both as an individual and as a member of a society.

Winners do not dedicated their lives to a concept of what they imagine they should be; rather, they are themselves and as such do not use their energy putting on a performance, maintaining pretence and manipulating others. They are aware that there is a difference between being loving and acting loving, between being stupid and acting stupid, between being knowledgeable and acting knowledgeable. Winners do not need to hide behind a mask.

Winners are not afraid to do their own thinking and to use their

---

"成者"与"败者"含义颇多。谈及成者我们并非指令他人失意之人。对我们而言，成者必为人守信，值得信赖，有求必应，态度诚恳，或为个人、或为社会一员皆能以真诚回应他人。

成者行事并不拘泥于某种信条，即便是他们认为应为其奉献一生的理念；而是本色行事，所以并不把精力用来表演，保持伪装或操控他人。他们明了爱与装爱、愚蠢与装傻、博学与卖弄之间迥然有别。成者无须藏于面具之后。

成者敢于利用所学，独立思考，区分事实与观点，并不佯装通晓所有

---

authentically *adv.* 确实地；真正地   trustworthy *adj* 可信赖的；可靠的

own knowledge. They can *separate* facts *from* opinions and don't pretend to have all the answers. They listen to others, evaluate what they say, but come to their own conclusions. Although winners can admire and respect other people, they are not totally defined, demolished, bound, or awed by them.

Winners do not play "helpless", nor do they play the blaming game. Instead, they assume responsibility for their own lives. They don't give others a false authority over them. Winners are their own bosses and know it.

A winner's timing is right. Winners respond *appropriately* to the situation. Their responses are related to the message sent and preserve the significance, worth, well-being, and dignity of the people involved. Winners know that for everything there is a season and for every activity a time.

答案。他们倾听、权衡他人意见，但能得出自己的结论。尽管他们尊重、敬佩他人，但并不为他人所局限、所推翻、所束缚，也不对他人敬若神灵。

成者既不佯装"无助"，也不抱怨他人。相反，他们对人生总是独担责任，也不以权威姿态凌驾他人之上。他们主宰自己，而且能意识到这点。

成者善于审时度势，随机应变。他们对所接受的信息做出回应，维护当事人的利益、康乐和尊严。成者深知一事要看好时节，行一事要把握时机。

---

separate from　区别　　　　　　　　appropriately　*adv.*　适当地

Although winners can freely enjoy themselves, they can also postpone enjoyment, can *discipline* themselves in the present to enhance their enjoyment in the future. Winners are not afraid to go after what he wants, but they do so in proper ways. Winners do not get their security by controlling others. They do not set themselves up to lose.

A winner cares about the world and its peoples. A winner is not isolated from the general problems of society, but is concerned, compassionate, and committed to improving the quality of life. Even in the face of national and international adversity, a winner's self-image is not one of a powerless *individual*. A winner works to make the world a better place.

尽管成者可以自由享乐，但他更知如何推迟享乐，适时自律，以期将来乐趣更胜。成者并不忌惮追求所想，但取之有道，也并不靠控制他人而获取安然之感。他们总是自己立于不败。

成者心忧天下，并不孤立于尘世弊病之外，而是置身事内，满腔热忱，致力于改善民生。即使面对民族、国家之危亡，成者亦非无力回天之体。他总是努力令世界更好。

discipline *v.* 磨炼　　　　　individual *n.* 个人；个体

41

Work and Pleasure

— Winston Churchill

To be really happy and really safe, one ought to have at least two or three hobbies, and they must all be real. It is no use starting late in life to say: "I will take an interest in this or that." Such an attempt only *aggravates* the strain of mental effort. A man may acquire great knowledge of topics unconnected with his

工作和娱乐
——温斯顿·丘吉尔

要想真正生活得幸福和平安，一个人至少应该有两三种业余爱好，而且必须是真正的爱好。到了晚年才开始说"我要培养这个或那个兴趣"是毫无用处的，这种尝试只会增加精神上的负担。在与自己日常工作无关的领域中，一个人可以获得渊博的知识，但却很难有所

aggravate v. 加重

daily work, and yet hardly get any benefit or relief. It is no use doing what you like; you have got to like what you do. *Broadly* speaking, human being may be divided into three classes: those who are toiled to death, those who are worried to death, and those who are bored to death. It is no use offering the manual laborer, tired out with a hard week's sweat and effort, the chance of playing a game of football or baseball on Saturday afternoon. It is no use inviting the politician or the professional or business man, who has been working or worrying about serious things for six days, to work or worry about trifling things at the weekend.

It may also be said that rational, industrious, useful human beings are divided into two classes: first, those whose work is work and whose pleasure is pleasure; and secondly, those whose work and pleasure are one. Of these the former are the majority. They have their *compensations*. The long hours in the office or the factory bring

---

收益或得到放松。做自己喜欢的事是无益的，你得喜欢自己所做的事。广言之，人可以分为三个类别：劳累而死的人，忧虑而死的人和无聊而死的人。对于那些体力劳动者来说，一周辛苦的工作使他们精疲力竭，因此在周六下午给他们提供踢足球或者打棒球的机会是没有意义的。对于政界人士，专业人士或者商人来说，他们已经为棘手的事务操劳或者烦恼了六天，因此在周末请他们为琐事劳神同样毫无意义。

　　或者可以这么说，理智的、勤奋的、有用的人可以分为两类：对第一类人而言，工作就是工作，娱乐就是娱乐；对于第二类人而言，工作和娱乐是合二为一的。很大一部分人属于前者。他们可以得到相应的补偿。在

---

broadly *adv.* 大体上　　　　　　　　　　compensation *n.* 补偿

with them as their reward, not only the means of *sustenance*, but a keen appetite for pleasure even in its simplest and most modest forms. But Fortune's favored children belong to the second class. Their life is a natural harmony. For them the working hours are never long enough. Each day is a holiday, and ordinary holidays when they come are grudged as enforced interruptions in an absorbing vacation. Yet to both classes the need of an alternative outlook, of a change of *atmosphere*, of a diversion of effort, is essential. Indeed, it may well be that those whose work is their pleasure are those who most need the means of banishing it at intervals from their minds.

办公室或工厂里长时间的工作，不仅带给他们维持生计的金钱，还带给他们一种渴求娱乐的强烈欲望，哪怕这种娱乐消遣是以最简单，最淳朴的方式进行的。而第二类人则是命运的宠儿。他们的生活自然而和谐。在他们看来，工作时间永远不够多，每天都是假期；而当正常的假日到来时，他们总会抱怨自己有趣的休假被强行中断。然而，有一些东西对于这两类人来说都十分必要，那就是变换一下视角，改变一下氛围，尝试做点不同的事情。事实上，那些把工作看作娱乐的人可能是需要以某种方式将工作不时地驱赶出自己的大脑。

---

sustenance *n.* 食物；营养   atmosphere *n.* 氛围

42

Gettysburg Address

— Abraham Lincoln

Four score and seven years ago our fathers brought forth on this continent a new nation, conceived in liberty and dedicated to the proposition that all men are created equal. Now we are *engaged in* a great civil war, testing whether that nation or any nation so conceived and so dedicated can long endure.

盖底斯堡演说

——亚伯拉罕·林肯

87年前，我们的先辈们在这个大陆上创立了一个新国家，它孕育于自由之中，奉行一切人生来平等的原则。现在我们正从事一场伟大的内战，以考验这个国家，或者任何一个孕育于自由和奉行上述原则的国家是否能够长久存在下去。

engage in 从事

We are met on a great battlefield of that war. We have come to dedicate a portion of that field as a final resting-place for those who here gave their lives that that nation might live. It is altogether fitting and proper that we should do this. But, in a larger sense, we cannot dedicate, we cannot *consecrate*, we cannot *hallow* this ground. The brave men, living and dead, who struggled here, have consecrated it far above our poor power to add or detract.

The world will little note nor long remember what we say here, but it can never forget what they did here. It is for us, the living, rather to be dedicated here to the unfinished work which they who fought here have thus far so nobly advanced. It is rather for us to be here

---

我们在这场战争中的一个伟大战场上集会。烈士们为使这个国家能够生存下去而献出了自己的生命，我们来到这里，是要把这个战场的一部分奉献给他们作为最后安息之所。我们这样做是完全应该而且是非常恰当的。但是，从更广泛的意义上来说，这块土地我们不能够奉献，不能够圣化，不能够神化。那些曾在这里战斗过的勇士们，活着的和去世的，已经把这块土地圣化了，这远不是我们微薄的力量所能增减的。

我们今天在这里所说的话，全世界不大会注意，也不会长久地记住，但勇士们在这里所做过的事，全世界却永远不会忘记。毋宁说，倒是我们这些还活着的人，应该在这里把自己奉献于勇士们已经如此崇高地向前推

---

consecrate v. 使圣化   hallow v. 使成为神圣

dedicated to the great task remaining before us——that from these honored dead we take increased *devotion* to that cause for which they gave the last full measure of devotion — that we here highly resolve that these dead shall not have died in vain, that this nation, under God, shall have a new birth of freedom, and that government of the people, by the people, for the people shall not perish from the earth.

进但尚未完成的事业。倒是我们应该在这里把自己奉献于仍然留在我们面前的伟大任务——我们要从这些光荣的死者身上汲取更多的献身精神，来完成他们已经完全彻底为之献身的事业；我们要在这里下定最大的决心，不让这些死者白白牺牲；我们要使国家在上帝福佑下得到自由的新生，要使这个民有、民治、民享的政府永世长存。

devotion *n.* 献身；奉献

43

Companionship of Books

— Samuel Smiles

A man may usually be known by the books he reads as well as by the company he keeps; for there is a companionship of books as well as of men; and one should always live in the best company, whether it be of books or of men.

A good book may be among the best of friends. It is the same today that it always

---

以书为伴

——塞缪尔·斯迈尔斯

通常看一人读些什么书就可知道他的为人，就像看他同什么人交往就可知道他的为人一样，因为有人以人为伴，也有人以书为伴。无论是书友还是朋友，我们都应该以最好的为伴。

好书就像是你最好的朋友。它始终不渝，过去如此，现在如此，将

---

was, and it will never change. It is the most patient and cheerful of companions. It does not turn its back upon us in times of adversity or *distress*. It always receives us with the same kindness; amusing and instructing us in youth, and comforting and consoling us in age.

Men often discover their *affinity* to each other by the mutual love they have for a book just as two persons sometimes discover a friend by the admiration which both entertain for a third. There is an old proverb, "Love me, love my dog." But there is more wisdom in this:" Love me, love my book." The book is a truer and higher bond of union. Men can think, feel, and *sympathize with* each other through their favorite author. They live in him together, and he in them.

来也永远不变。它是最有耐心，最令人愉悦的伴侣。在我们穷愁潦倒，临危遭难时，它也不会抛弃我们，对我们总是一如既往地亲切。在我们年轻时，好书陶冶我们的性情，增长我们的知识；到我们年老时，它又给我们以慰藉和勉励。

人们常常因为喜欢同一本书而结为知己，就像有时两个人因为敬慕同一个人而成为朋友一样。有句古谚说道："爱屋及乌。"其实"爱我及书"这句话蕴涵更多的哲理。书是更为真诚而高尚的情谊纽带。人们可以通过共同喜爱的作家沟通思想，交流感情，彼此息息相通，并与自己喜欢的作家思想相通，情感相融。

distress *n.* 痛苦　　　　affinity *n.* 亲近
sympathize with 同情；对……赞同

A good book is often the best urn of a life enshrining the best that life could think out; for the world of a man's life is, for the most part, but the world of his thoughts. Thus the best books are treasuries of good words, the golden thoughts, which, remembered and cherished, become our constant companions and comforters.

Books possess an essence of *immortality*. They are by far the most lasting products of human effort. Temples and statues decay, but books survive. Time is of no account with great thoughts, which are as fresh today as when they first passed through their author's minds, ages ago. What was then said and thought still speaks to us as *vividly* as ever from the printed page. The only effect of time have been to sift out the bad products; for nothing in literature can long survive but what is really good.

好书常如最精美的宝器，珍藏着人生思想的精华，因为人生的境界主要就在于其思想的境界。因此，最好的书是金玉良言和崇高思想的宝库，这些良言和思想若铭记于心并多加珍视，就会成为我们忠实的伴侣和永恒的慰藉。

书籍具有不朽的本质，是为人类努力创造的最为持久的成果。寺庙会倒塌，神像会朽烂，而书却经久长存。对于伟大的思想来说，时间是无关紧要的。多年前初次闪现于作者脑海的伟大思想今日依然清新如故。时间唯一的作用是淘汰不好的作品，因为只有真正的佳作才能经世长存。

---

immortality *n.* 不朽　　　　　　　　vividly *adv.* 生动地；逼真地

Books introduce us into the best society; they bring us into the presence of the greatest minds that have ever lived. We hear what they said and did; we see the as if they were really alive; we sympathize with them, enjoy with them, grieve with them; their experience becomes ours, and we feel as if we were in a measure actors with them in the scenes which they describe.

The great and good do not die, even in this world. *Embalmed* in books, their spirits walk abroad. The book is a living voice. It is an intellect to which on still listens.

书籍介绍我们与最优秀的人为伍，使我们置身于历代伟人巨匠之间，如闻其声，如观其行，如见其人，同他们情感交融，悲喜与共，感同身受。我们觉得自己仿佛在作者所描绘的舞台上和他们一起粉墨登场。

即使在人世间，伟大杰出的人物也永生不死。他们的精神被载入书册，传于四海。书是人生至今仍在聆听的智慧之声，永远充满着活力。

---

embalm *v.* （尸体）进行防腐处理

44

Blood, Toil, Tears and Sweat

— Winston Churchill

I would say to the House, as I said to those who have joined this government: "I have nothing to offer but blood, toil, tears and sweat."

We have before us an *ordeal* of the most grievous kind. We have before us many, many long months of struggle and of suffering. You ask, what is our policy? I can say: It

热血、辛劳、眼泪和汗水

——温斯顿·丘吉尔

正如我曾对参加本届政府的成员所说的那样，我要对下院说："我没什么可以奉献，有的只是热血、辛劳、眼泪和汗水。"

摆在我们面前的，是一场极为痛苦严峻的考验。在我们面前，有许多许多漫长的斗争和苦难的岁月。你们问：我们的政策是什么？我要说，在海上、陆地和空中进行战争。我们的政策就是用我们全部能力，用上帝所

---

ordeal *n.* 煎熬；磨难

is to wage war, by sea, land and air, with all our might and with all the strength that God can give us; to wage war against a *monstrous tyranny*, never surpassed in the dark, *lamentable* catalogue of human crime. That is our policy. You ask, what is our aim? I can answer in one word: It is victory, victory at all costs, victory in spite of all terror, victory, however long and hard the road may be; for without victory, there is no survival. Let that be realized; no survival for the British Empire, no survival for all that the British Empire has stood for, no survival for the urge and impulse of the ages, that mankind will move forward towards its goal. But I take up my task with *buoyancy* and hope. I feel sure that our cause will not be suffered to fail among men. At this time I feel entitled to claim the aid of all, and I say, "Come then, let us go forward together with our united strength."

给予我们的全部力量，同一个在人类黑暗悲惨的罪恶史上所从未有过的穷凶极恶的暴政进行战争。这就是我们的政策。你们问：我们的目标是什么？我可以用一个词来回答：那就是胜利。不惜一切代价，去赢得胜利；无论多么可怕，也要赢得胜利，无论道路多么遥远和艰难，也要赢得胜利，因为没有胜利，就不能生存。大家必须认识到这一点：没有英帝国的存在，就没有英帝国所代表的一切，就没有促使人类朝着自己目标奋勇前进这一世代相传的强烈欲望和动力。但是当我挑起这个担子的时候，我是心情愉快、满怀希望的。我深信，人们不会听任我们的事业遭受失败。此时此刻，我觉得我有权利要求大家的支持，我要说："来吧，让我们同心协力，一道前进。"

monstrous *adj.* 极不公正的
lamentable *adj.* 使人惋惜的

tyranny *n.* 暴政
buoyancy *n.* 乐观；愉快的心情

45

The Road of Life

— William.S.Maugham

The lives of most men are determined by their environment. They accept the circumstances amid which fate has thrown them not only with resignation but even with good will. They are like streetcars running contentedly on their rails and they despise the sprightly flitter that dashes in and out of the traffic

生活之路

——威廉·S·毛姆

大多数人的生活都是由他们所处的环境决定。他们顺从地甚至乐意地接受命运把他们所扔进的环境。他们就像电车一样满足地行驶于他们的轨道上，并且瞧不起那些在敏捷地出没车水马龙中，快乐地

and speeds so *jauntily* across the open country. I respect them; they are good citizens, good husbands, and good fathers, and of course somebody has to pay the taxes; but I do not find them exciting. I am fascinated by the men, few enough in all conscience, who take life in their own hands and seem to *mould* it to their own liking. It maybe that we have no such a thing as free will, but at all events, we have the *illusion* of it. At a cross-road it does seem to us that we might go either to the right or the left and, the choice once made, it is difficult to see that the whole course of the world's history obliged us to take the turning we did.

奔驰于旷野上的车子。我尊重他们，他们是好公民、好丈夫和好父亲，当然总得要有人来交税。但是，他们并没有令人兴奋的地方。我被另外一些人深深吸引，他们将命运掌握在自己手中，并且似乎把它改造成他们所喜欢的样子，这样的人是很少的。而或许我们并没有所谓的自由意志，但不管怎样我们总有那样的幻觉。在一个十字路口前，似乎我们可以走这条路也可以走那一条路，不过一旦做出选择，我们很难意识到其实是整个世界历史进程迫使我们选择那个方向的。

---

jauntily *adj.* 精力充沛的

illusion *n.* 错觉；幻想

mould *v.* 塑造；改变

46

Clear Your Mental Space
—— by Anonymous

Think about the last time you felt a negative emotion—like stress, anger, or frustration. What was going through your mind as you were going through that *negativity*? Was your mind cluttered with thoughts? Or was it paralyzed, unable to think?

The next time you find yourself in the

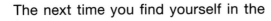

清理心灵的空间
——佚名

想下你最近一次感受到的消极情绪，例如压力，愤怒或挫折。当你处于那种消极情绪时你在想些什么？是充满了混乱的思绪？还是陷于麻木，无法思考？

下次当你发现自己处于非常紧张的状态时，或是你感到气愤或受挫

---

negativity *n.* 消极性

middle of a very stressful time, or you feel angry or *frustrated*, stop. Yes, that's right, stop. Whatever you're doing, stop and sit for one minute. While you're sitting there, completely immerse yourself in the negative emotion.

Allow that emotion to consume you. Allow yourself one minute to truly feel that emotion. Don't cheat yourself here. Take the entire minute—but only one minute—to do nothing else but feel that emotion.

When the minute is over, ask yourself, "Am I wiling to keep holding on to this negative emotion as I go through the rest of the day?"

Once you've allowed yourself to be totally immersed in the emotion and really fell it, you will be surprised to find that the

---

时，停下来。是的，对，停下来。不管你在做什么，停下来坐上一分钟。坐着的时候，让自己完全沉浸在那种消极情绪之中。

让那种消极情绪吞噬你，给自己一分钟的时间去真切地体会那种情绪，不要欺骗自己。花整整一分钟的时间 —— 但只有一分钟 —— 去体会那种情绪，别的什么也不要做。

当一分钟结束时，问自己："我是否想在今天余下的时间里继续保持这种消极情绪？"

一旦你允许自己完全沉浸在那种情绪当中并真切体会到它，你就会惊奇地发现那种情绪很快就消失了。

---

frustrated *adj.* 沮丧的

emotion clears rather quickly.

If you feel you need to hold on to the emotion for a little longer, that is OK. Allow yourself another minute to feel the emotion.

When you feel you've had enough of the emotion, ask yourself if you're willing to carry that negativity with you for the rest of the day. If not, *take a deep breath*. As you *exhale*, release all that negativity with your breath.

This exercise seems simple—almost too simple. But, it is very *effective*. By allowing that negative emotion the space to be truly felt, you are *dealing with* the emotion rather than stuffing it down and trying not to feel it. You are actually taking away the power of the emotion by giving it the space and attention it needs. When you immerse yourself in the emotion, and realize that it is only emotion, it loses its control. You can clear your head and proceed with your

---

如果你觉得还需要点时间来保持那种情绪，没关系，再给自己一分钟的时间去体会它。

如果你觉得自己已经充分体会了那种情绪，那就问自己是否愿意在今天余下的时间里继续保持这种消极情绪。如果不愿意，那就深呼吸。呼气的时候，把所有的消极情绪都释放出去。

这个方法似乎很简单 —— 几乎是太过简单了，但却非常有效。通过给自己空间真正体会消极情绪，你是在处理这种情绪，而不是将其压制下去然后尽量不加理会。通过给予消极情绪所需的空间和关注，你实际上是在消解其力量。当你沉浸在那种情绪之中，并且明白它只是一种情绪时，你就摆脱了它的控制。你可以清理头脑并继续做事。

---

take a deep breath　深吸气

effective *adj.* 有效的

exhale *v.* 呼气

deal with　处理

task.

Try it. Next time you're in the middle of a negative emotion, give yourself the space to feel the emotion and see what happens. Keep a piece of paper with you that says the following:

Stop. Immerse for one minute. Do I want to keep this negativity? Breath deep, exhale, release. Move on!

This will remind you of the steps to the process. Remember; take the time you need to really immerse yourself in the emotion. Then, when you feel you've felt it enough, release it—really let go of it. You will be surprised at how quickly you can move on from a negative *situation* and get to what you really want to do!

你下次笼罩消极情绪时，试一下这种做法，给自己一点空间来体会那种情绪并看看会发生什么。随身带一张写着如下字句的纸条：

停下来。沉浸一分钟。我想保持这种消极情绪吗？深吸气，呼气，放松。继续做事！

这会提醒你该怎样去做。记住，要花你所需要的时间去真正沉浸于那种情绪之中。然后，当你感到自己已经充分体会到了它。你会惊奇地发现，你很快就能摆脱消极情绪，并开始做你真正想做的事情！

situation *n.* 情况

47

A White Wild Rose

— Bing Xin

Why was I standing alone by the riverside? *Twilight* dim, was it dawn or dusk? Nowhere could I get replied, and I felt as if what appeared before me were just a world of flowers, among which were scattered several white wild roses. She came. She came down from the mountain, *dressed up* attractively,

---

一朵白蔷薇

——冰心

怎么独自站在河边上？这朦胧的天色，是黎明还是黄昏？何处询问，只觉得眼前竟是花的世界。中间杂着几朵白蔷薇。她来了，她从山上下来了。靓妆着，仿佛是一身缟白，手里抱着一大束花。我

---

twilight *n.* 黄昏   dress up 打扮

as if all in white, with a big bunch of flowers in her hands. I said, "Come. I'll give you a white wild rose to clasp on the hem", She said something with a smile but too faintly to be caught. However, most probably I didn't pick any white wild rose and she didn't wear it. She headed forward with her flowers still in her hands.

Raising my eyes towards the path she'd just covered, I could see nothing along its sides but flowers *in full bloom*, flowers hanging low and flowers fallen to the ground. Anyhow, white flowers are better than red ones, I think—but, why didn't I pick and why didn't she wear any? What place is the road ahead and why didn't I follow her steps? All is gone: the flowers are nowhere to be seen and the dream is already over. How about the road ahead? Even if picked, could the white wild rose be worn?

(Written afterwards on August 20, 1921)

说，"你来，给你一朵白蔷薇，好簪在襟上。"她微笑说了一句话，只是听不见。然而似乎我竟没有摘，她也没有戴，依旧抱着花儿，向前走了。

抬头望她去路，只见得两旁开满了花，垂满了花，落满了花。我想白花终比红花好；然而为何我竟没有摘，她也竟没有戴？前路是什么地方，为何不随她走去？都过去了，花也隐了，梦也醒了，前路如何？便摘也何曾戴？

1921年8月20日追记。

---

in full bloom   正在开花